Steph
m
ther in
Crime!
- D -
Ash

hum♥R
for a
sister's heart

Stories, Quips, and Quotes
to Lift the Heart

hum♥r
for a
sister's heart

Patsy Clairmont • Martha Bolton • Karen Scalf Linamen

Susan Duke • Marti Attoun • and many more

HOWARD BOOKS
A DIVISION OF SIMON & SCHUSTER
New York   London   Toronto   Sydney

Compiled by Snapdragon Group℠ Editorial Services

Illustrated by Dennis Hill

Our purpose at Howard Books is to:
- *Increase faith* in the hearts of growing Christians
- *Inspire holiness* in the lives of believers
- *Instill hope* in the hearts of struggling people everywhere

Because He's coming again!

 Howard Books, a division of Simon & Schuster, Inc.
1230 Avenue of the Americas, New York, NY 10020

ISBN: 978-0-7394-9149-2

Interior Design by John Mark Luke Designs

Contents

Chapter 3: Sisters Are the Perfect Accessory for Life

Chapter 4: Sisters Are Born for Adventure

Chapter 5: Sisters Make Good Leaning Posts

Chapter 6: Sisters Are Familiar Strangers

Chapter 7: Sisters Were Created to Teach Us Patience

Chapter 8: Sisters Reside in a Town Called Disaster

Chapter 9: Sisters Are Always in Your Hair

Chapter 1

Sisters Are There for You in a Pinch

No Friend Like a Sister

There is no friend like a sister.
In calm and stormy weather;
To cheer one on the tedious way,
To fetch one if one goes astray.
To lift one if one totters down,
To strengthen whilst one stands.

—CHRISTINA ROSSETTI

Make My Day, Doughboy!

Karen Scalf Linamen

For some unknown reason, I was awake at 3 a.m. when my sister Michelle tiptoed past my bedroom door. I said, "Hey."

"Hey back." She poked her head in my room. "I'm glad you're awake. I heard a noise in the basement."

Ten months earlier, my two kids and I moved into a big old house in the woods and invited my sister and five-year-old niece to move in with us. No husbands or sons, just two single moms, our three daughters, and enough clothes to fashionably outfit a third-world country. Now the dark basement of that big old house was making weird noises in the middle of the night.

I threw on a robe and we tiptoed down the stairs, through the main hall, around the corner, and peered down the basement stairwell.

I whispered, "What did you hear?"

"I heard scratching. It was so loud I thought it was you."

I frowned. "Just how loud do I scratch?"

"I think we need a weapon."

"Curling iron? Stilletos? Cheez Whiz?"

Michelle smacked palm to forehead. "Gun!"

Michelle's former husband, Russ, had been a police officer. Of course there would be a gun. I followed her into the office and watched as she tried to remember the combination to the fire safe. Eventually she gave up, rocked back on her heels, and looked at me. At the exact same moment we both said, "Rolling pins!"

It's amazing we even own rolling pins. After all, we *are* a household run by two single moms. We don't have husbands to keep in line, and we don't have time to bake from scratch. Nevertheless, five minutes later we were armed and dangerous.

It's amazing we even own rolling pins. After all, we are a household run by two single moms.

Michelle said it well. Brandishing her rolling pin she shouted, "Hey, whoever you are—we're armed and dangerous!"

I sighed. "The Pillsbury Doughboy is quaking in his boots. Look, maybe we should call the police. Sure, we could go down together into the dark basement, clutching each other, flashlight in one hand and rolling pin in the other, but, frankly, I've seen those movies and it never ends well."

She saw my point. We called 911, and ten minutes later we spotted flashlight beams darting around the house. When we answered a rap at the door, three officers filled the hallway. Michelle told them what she'd heard, and they disappeared into the bowels of the house.

We waited.

I sat cross-legged on the floor of the hall in my terry-cloth robe. Michelle sat on the bottom step of the stairs leading to the bedrooms where our daughters slept soundly. There were three men in our basement. Four if you counted the intruder. Or maybe three men and a squirrel. Michelle was still holding the rolling pin and wearing fuzzy slippers. Now that we no longer needed to protect our children with a baking implement, this suddenly seemed like an awfully exciting thing to be doing at 3:42 a.m. Adrenaline high and danger on the wane, we began to giggle.

I admitted, "I called the police once like this when I was living in California. I kept hearing noises on the porch. The cop searched the outside of the house for ten minutes, then rang the bell to give me the news. Turns out I'd put a bag of trash on the front porch and some animal had been digging through it. Boy, did I feel stupid."

Michelle laughed. "When Russ was a rookie cop, he was doing a patrol check on a vacant house that was under construction, when he *really* had to pee. The plumbing was working, but none of the rooms had doors yet. As he's standing there taking care of business, it dawns on him that someone could sneak up behind him, so he draws his gun. Sure enough, he hears something behind him and whips around, a gun in one hand and, well . . . let's just say he had both hands full. I guarantee *that* electrician will think twice before showing up early for work ever again!"

We laughed, exchanged more stories, laughed until we cried. We hadn't howled like this in months.

Michelle and I grew up happily together in Downey, California. Six years apart, we had rarely argued and were the best of friends. Moving in together twenty years later as adults should have felt

familiar and predictable. Instead, the transition had proven a little more interesting than that. As it turns out, Michelle enjoys planning ahead while I, more often than not, am flying by the seat of my pants. She loves lunches downtown while I prefer grilled cheese at home. She likes to plan intimate soirees with close friends, while I regularly invite hordes of acquaintances to drop in anytime they're in the state of Colorado.

Circumstantial stress had taken its toll as well: We'd each had our hearts broken. Finances had been tight. Merging two households into one had been a major undertaking. And on top of everything else, our old house in the woods kept handing us interesting challenges like a flooded basement, beehives by the front door, and cell phone reception so unreliable as to be considered a myth by many who knew us.

Yep, we hadn't laughed like this in a very long time.

Eventually the officers reappeared to report that our basement was secure. They had no idea what Michelle had heard, but they were certain we were safe. They returned to their beat, and Michelle and I returned, lighter-hearted, to our beds.

Still—

Whenever life throws me a curve, whenever I feel tired or discouraged or alone, I think of an image from that night and I have to laugh.

It's the image of two sisters clutching each other, walking bravely into the unknown—pointing a flashlight into the darkness and waving rolling pins. After all, sometimes things go bump in the night. Sometimes they go bump in your life. A sister by your side can make all the difference in the world. The fuzzy slippers are optional.

Mad About Mood Rings

Cathy Lee Phillips

Bertha. The world knows the name. Military annals remember Big Bertha as a weapon crucial to Germany during World War I, a sort of Howitzer on wheels. Golfers know her as a Callaway titanium driver. Helicopters bearing her name have zigzagged the skies while, in 1996, Category 3 Hurricane Bertha pulverized Puerto Rico and the Virgin Islands.

During the recent holidays my sister, Merrie, and I reminisced about the Bertha in our own lives—our grandmother on our mama's side. Some called her Granny; some called her difficult; others called her unique. In fact, she had so many colorful nicknames (use your imagination!) that I actually didn't know her name was Bertha until I was fourteen.

Call her what you will, Bertha was a force in my life. She was the first to teach me that the face someone wore on Sunday was not necessarily the face they wore on weekdays. She was a multitasker

who could quote Scripture, read an article from *Guideposts,* and gossip with gusto all at the same time. She was healthy as a horse, but instead of being thankful, she traveled from doctor to doctor seeking an ailment she could share with the other little old ladies. She never left her home state of Georgia or studied current events, yet her opinions on all topics national and international were expected to be shared by her family.

"Remember," she would say, "I am the matriarch!"

Contact with Bertha was usually limited to Easter, Thanksgiving, Christmas, and her birthday. Occasionally, though, she decided to visit our house, an occurrence that stirred fear in the hearts of folks within a twenty-mile radius of Posey Road. Neighbors wouldn't visit, friends wouldn't call, cows wouldn't give milk, and I swear the flowers wilted. This wasn't just a visit. It was more like a biblical plague, with Bertha playing the parts of both the locusts and frogs.

Merrie and I were on the front lines during Bertha's visits. We were kids who never pleased her. Plus, we despised the chicken and dumplings she somehow decided we loved. Within minutes of her arrival, a bottomless pot of those soggy things simmered on our GE range. Bertha's other culinary specialty was steak and gravy, which we liked but never got. That dish was reserved for Bertha's eldest daughter, the one with the bigger house. According to Bertha, our family "just seemed more chicken people than steak people." We were too young then to realize we had been insulted.

While the dumplings dumpled, Bertha unpacked her vast collection of powders, creams, and beauty supplies. She put away her *unmentionables,* a word she used to mention underwear without

mentioning underwear. We had never seen anything like them. They were panties with legs, sort of large nylon Bermuda shorts. Though unmentionable, they were suitable for public viewing when Bertha hung them out to dry. Merrie and I hid behind the well house and giggled for hours watching those big old Bertha Britches boogie in the breeze.

Bertha spent far more than her fair share of time in our one bathroom. And once she left, we were afraid to go back in. One late night, Merrie stumbled half-asleep into the bathroom to do what came naturally. Once she shut the door, she spotted a set of teeth—without an owner—soaking inside a clear glass. Forty years later, I can still hear the scream, and Merrie is still having denture-related nightmares.

She put away her unmentionables, a word she used to mention underwear without mentioning underwear.

Bertha, though, outdid herself during Christmas 1970. Like most every young girl in America that year, Merrie and I desperately wanted a Partridge Family album. Back then albums cost anywhere from six to eight dollars (*album—a large, round, black object, which, when a needle was applied, played music; predecessor of the eight-track, cassette tape, and CD*).

However, on Christmas morning 1970, there was no Partridge Family album under our tree, but we sure heard one playing in Cousin Wanda Lou's room when we arrived at her house for Christmas dinner. Wanda Lou's house was party central for all the family celebrations because it was much bigger and nicer than

our house. Wanda Lou had her own room with a beanbag chair, Donny Osmond posters, and even a black light! Obviously, they were rich beyond our imagination.

Wanda Lou invited Merrie and me upstairs and actually let us hold her precious album while she displayed all the other goodies Santa left under her tree. We may have smiled politely but, let me tell you, we coveted our cousin's Partridge Family album. Then she offered words of hope: "Granny gave it to me."

Bertha? Bertha bought a Partridge Family album? Perhaps if she bought one for Wanda Lou she would have bought one for all her grandchildren. It would be only right and fair and nondiscriminatory.

As we sat near the Christmas tree after dinner, Merrie and I were each given a small package from Bertha, far too small to hold a Partridge Family album.

"Maybe there's money inside so we can buy our own album," Merrie whispered.

We clawed away the paper and opened our little boxes. There were no bills. No gift certificates to a record store. There were . . . please tell me I'm hallucinating . . . this can't be true . . . mood rings. Each box held a little mood ring, a 1970s classic piece of round glass on an adjustable ring. The glass supposedly changed colors with your mood. Mood rings! The only thing that changed color was the skin on my finger when I wore the thing.

"Hey, I saw these stupid things at Woolworth's last week, and they were three for a dollar," Merrie hissed.

"Well, my doggone mood ring is going to be black the rest of the day," I hissed back.

Wanda Lou grinned from her spot next to the sparkling tree. It was obvious. Bertha liked Wanda Lou more than she liked us. What a stupid world.

I was willing to let things go, but Merrie has always had a temper worse than a rattlesnake with a hangover. So I wasn't too surprised when just before leaving, she cornered Bertha.

"So, Granny, why did you give Wanda Lou a Partridge Family album when all you gave me and Cathy was a thirty-three-cent mood ring?"

Shocked at being confronted, Bertha cleared her throat several times. "Well, Merrie Sue (knowing full well that my sister hated being called by both her first and middle names), Wanda Lou's family has more money, and she is used to better things. I always get her something nicer."

"Well, that's about the dumbest thing I ever heard!" Merrie snapped. She would still be talking to this very day if Mama hadn't shoved her into the car. We ranted nonstop about mood rings and life's unfairness during our seventy-mile trip home. We couldn't believe that even Bertha could have such an attitude.

Merrie and I laughed about those mood rings this Christmas. We know how silly it is to fret over a thirty-three-cent gift, though we still feel the sting of being the "lesser" children, financially speaking. We grew up tough, but we grew up wise. And wisdom and faith have taught me that the precious gift of Christmas is not reserved for those who have always had the nicer things. God gave His very best, and the love of that baby of Bethlehem is offered equally to everyone. *Whosoever*, says John 3:16. And by knowing the love of Christ, we should seek to treat all people

with worth and dignity—those people whose behavior makes us gasp, even everyday people like you . . . like me.

Jesus, born in a stable, cradled in hay and surrounded by animals, started out as a farm kid like Merrie and me. He wasn't born into the richest family, but the wise men knew to bring Him gold.

No doubt Bertha would have brought chicken, dumplings, and a lovely mood ring.

Get Back in the Saddle, Missy!

Dandi Daley Mackall

Sometimes it's hard to believe my sister and I swim in the same gene pool. Only our voices are the same—our own mother can't tell us apart on the phone. Maureen, the older sister by three years, is blonde and blue-eyed. I'm a brown-eyed brunette. Maureen loves shopping, watches soap operas, and does lunch. I hate shopping, read mysteries, and eat whatever is closest to the computer.

When we were kids, I climbed trees and played baseball, while Maureen baked cookies and played with dolls. Yet one thing kept us close—horses. And long after our childhood horses had gone to that Great Pasture in the Sky, what we learned on horseback kept my sister and me together. We had one rule we followed, no matter what: *If you fall off your horse, you have to get back in the saddle, Missy.* I suppose we picked it up from *Bonanza* or *Wagon Train,* because we rarely rode with saddles. Saddles were too much

trouble when you were itching to ride a country lane before the sun beat you to it. Or when you just went to the pasture to hay the horses, but couldn't resist jumping on bareback with nothing but a rope and a halter.

Like the Saturday we walked to the pasture and fed Maureen's buckskin mare, Rocket, and my black Misty. Maureen bridled Rocket, but all I had for Misty was his halter. It was enough to get me to jump aboard and hope Misty would let me steer with my legs.

Our biggest fear was that a fall might make one of us afraid to ride again.

Maureen and Rocket took off toward the pond, and Misty and I followed. But Misty kept gaining speed, and there wasn't much I could do about it. He took a turn uphill and headed for the trees. I held on until we hit low-hanging willows. Their branches swept over me, sending me tumbling like sagebrush down to the edge of the pond.

"Dandi! You okay?" Maureen shouted down.

I was scraped, but not broken. "I'm okay."

Maureen disappeared, then returned with my horse. "Get back in the saddle, Missy!" she shouted.

Our biggest fear was that a fall might make one of us afraid to ride again. I hauled myself up the hill, where my sister waited next to my horse, her hands cupped into a stirrup, ready to boost me up. In minutes, we were cantering the back pasture.

A few years later, I returned the favor. I was still riding Misty bareback, but Maureen had switched to a nice quarter horse

named Ash Bill. We were out riding on a hot summer's day, when a dog barked, or a car backfired, and Bill let loose with a series of bucks that sent Maureen flying.

I caught Bill, then checked on my sister.

"I think I'm hurt," she said, struggling to her feet, holding her arm funny.

I slid off Misty and cupped my hands for a stirrup to help Maureen back up into the saddle. But Maureen shook her head. Maureen hadn't ridden much that summer. She'd decided boys were more interesting than horses.

I wasn't ready to lose her, though. Not yet. "Get back in the saddle, Missy."

For minutes, neither of us budged. I stayed bent over with my stirrup-hands. She stood still, holding her arm. Finally, she stepped up, wincing, and got back on her horse.

I held the horses while our dad, the town's only doctor, x-rayed Maureen's arm. It was broken. I let her ride home in the car with Dad.

The next year, Maureen stopped riding—not because of a fall, but because of Butch. Butch was a notorious two-timer, a fact known to everyone in high school, except my sister. If I'd been a brother, instead of sister, we might have had a *High Noon* situation.

Then opportunity knocked. Maureen had turned down my invitation to go riding, again, because Butch was dropping by. But when I got back, he hadn't come, and Maureen was listening to "Lara's Theme" from *Dr. Zhivago*. Never a good sign. My parents, picking up on the sad music, involved my sister in a backyard barbecue while I cleaned up.

The phone rang, and I answered it.

"Maureen, are you mad?" It was Butch.

Some things had changed with my sister and me over the years, but our voices had not. "What do *you* think?" I demanded. "You stood me up! Was it Linda this time?"

Butch was momentarily speechless.

I was not. "I know all about you and Linda."

"She means nothing to me, babe!" he insisted.

"And *you* mean nothing to me. Butch, we are over!" I slammed down the receiver, giddy with the realization that I had just broken up with my sister's cheating boyfriend.

Maureen stayed broken up with Butch for about twenty-four hours, until the truth came out and I got grounded. Still, a month later, when *he* broke up with *her,* I'm the one she came to. "I will never date again," she vowed.

I listened for a while. Then I said, "Sometimes you have to trade in the horse, but you can't give up riding. Get back in the saddle, Missy."

We laughed hard.

Since then, I've had my share of falls—some from horses, some from life. What a blessing it's been to have a sister who would tell me, "Get back in the saddle, Missy," and cup her hands into a stirrup when I've needed one.

In the Clutches of Summer

Marti Attoun

As we neared Florida and some relatives that my eleven-year-old son had never met, he mumbled the question that he'd been mulling for many miles.

"I wonder if they're huggers?"

I could have lied and said that, after traveling twelve hundred miles, we'd probably all greet each other by saluting. Worse, I could have told the truth—that someday he, too, would convert from huggee to hugger. I didn't want him to gag, though.

"Yes, it's possible that you'll be hugged," I warned. "Just hold your breath and think about something good—like summer."

Every family harbors some dyed-in-the-wool huggers who mark arrivals and departures with enthusiastic squeezes. The grown-ups never seem to notice or be bothered; the kids always do.

My childhood summers were framed by the arms of the huggers who visited from western Kansas each year. As soon as Mom

announced that Uncle Jim and Aunt Nadine were on the horizon, my sisters and I would giggle and plot our strategy as we camped on the divan. It was a tan three-piece sectional, which Mom frequently divided and shuffled around the room. We strategically occupied one slice.

I was locked against her bosom, suddenly as vast as western Kansas, waiting for her to stop patting my back so I could exhale.

"I'm going first to get it over with," my sister Rose would whisper.

"Maybe they'll be talking up a blue streak with Mom and won't notice us," Winnie would say.

Mom knew exactly what we were up to. "Now, girls, be nice," she'd say. "You haven't seen Uncle Jim and Aunt Nadine since last summer."

Of course, we would be nice. But how could one tiny woman, no bigger than a blue jay, have arms that stretched longer than our living room?

The minute Mom heard their car tires crunch the gravel driveway, she was out the door. Uncle Jim's laughter floated across the front yard and spilled onto the porch and into the house.

And there they stood. Aunt Nadine peeled her pocketbook off her arm and set it on the TV. The two of them beamed at us, arms wide open and empty.

Uncle Jim scooped up Rose. Then Aunt Nadine squealed at me, "Come here, you little sweetie pie."

There's no escaping, I told myself. It's the spinach of summer. Slurp it down; then you're finished until the next visit. I inched off the divan.

Aunt Nadine swooped me into her arms, which smelled like lemon bath powder. "I'd like to squeeze the stuffin' out of you, you little dickens," she said. "Just look how big you've grown."

I couldn't look. I was locked against her bosom, suddenly as vast as western Kansas, waiting for her to stop patting my back so I could exhale. After forever, she released me, and I swapped places with Rose.

We three huggees giggled after this ritual. Finally, summer had officially arrived.

Any Port in a Storm

Brenda Nixon

As a little girl, my older sister, Lee Lee, was my role model. I looked to her for important lessons like how to play with Barbie, primp in the mirror, and match my outfits. In the summers, we went to vacation Bible school together and rode our bikes around the neighborhood until dark. During the school year, I'd try to carry my books smugly like Lee Lee—she always seemed so smart. I was the tagalong little sib who followed her and her friends door-to-door for trick or treat and to school plays and carnivals. Sometimes we fought, and more objects flew around the house than alien spaceships in Roswell, New Mexico.

The best part of growing up with Lee Lee was sharing a tiny bedroom with her in our modest suburban home. Our twin beds lay parallel so we could see each other as our heads rested on our pillows. In my young mind, it was comforting to sleep in the same room with my bigger, wiser, older sister. Every evening after

Mom tucked us into bed and turned out the lights, we chattered and giggled until drowsiness—or Mom—descended and we whispered our final goodnight.

One March evening, a harsh spring thunderstorm interrupted our sleep. Sharp lightning exposed creepy shadows on the walls. Rolling thunder vibrated the windows like an imprisoned monster shaking the bars in his cell. Silently I huddled, concentrating on the tempest and wondering, *How can Mom and Dad*

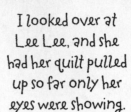

I looked over at Lee Lee, and she had her quilt pulled up so far only her eyes were showing.

stay asleep? Then, during the clamor, came a momentary calm and Lee Lee whispered over to me, "Brenda, are you scared?"

"No," I truthfully answered.

A pause, thunder crashed, then . . .

"Are you sure?"

"I'm sure."

Another pause. I looked over at Lee Lee, and she had her quilt pulled up so far only her eyes were showing.

More thunder. A brilliant flash of lightning.

"You want me to get in bed with you?"

"No. I'm fine, really," I insisted.

In the morning she was lying beside me in my bed, sound asleep, so close that her hair tickled the back of my neck.

Lee Lee's so-called benevolent act still brings a smile to my face and the slightest hint of a chuckle. That bigger, wiser, older sister of mine, my precious Lee Lee, apparently wasn't so much braver!

"Brief" Shopping Mission
Marti Attoun

My sister, Winnie, just spent two hours marooned in the men's underwear department while I sat enthroned in the mall food court. I considered filing a missing sister's report.

Suddenly, after five decades of wearing the same brand of men's briefs from the local discounter, my brother-in-law Dan announced that he needed to upgrade. Maybe it's a postmidlife crisis. Who knows what triggers a perfectly predictable person to wake up one morning and want to upgrade his underwear?

At any rate, the waistbands on the cheapies had developed a bad habit of detaching themselves from the rest of their party. After a few trips through the bleach, the briefs were being demoted to dust rags.

"Just grab me a three-pack of the better men's briefs when you're at Macy's," Dan said.

This sounds like a simple mission, but there was nothing brief about her underwear-buying adventure. The experience was akin to buying a car. Each designer had his own model and each model had its own designs. So many styles, options, colors, and fabrics. A smart shopper would consult *Consumer Reports* first.

Do you want the high-rise, low-rise, mid-thigh boxers, button-fly, Banlon, cotton, polyester, or silk? Do you want the S, M, L, XL or the ones that are measured by waist size? Fluorescent, or Mickey Mouse print?

Do you want the high-rise, low-rise, mid-thigh boxers, button-fly, Banlon, cotton, polyester, or silk?

From the looks of things, yesteryear's bland skivvies are going the way of feed sack and burlap underwear. Soon you'll only be able to find these models at garage sales, and that's going to be a bit awkward for some of these old geezers.

I can imagine a grizzled garage saler. "You got any fishin' tackle or pocketknives . . . or plain white men's unmentionables?"

By the time Winnie decided on some single packs of Perry Ellis boxers for $14.50 each, she looked as frazzled as Dan's dust rags.

"These were expensive, but I've had it," she said, and collapsed over a Chinese eggroll and a slab of Italian pizza. "They're modest and have a seam-free waistband that's nonbinding. There's no elastic in the waistband to unravel and they should fit over his big gut."

The next morning, she called with an update.

"Dan put on his new underwear this morning and I heard him hollering," she said. "He thought he had them on backward."

She had considered all the options, except one. This modern model didn't have a fly.

"I told him that I'm not battling mall shoppers another day," she said. "He can get out his pocketknife and whittle on them to suit himself."

Chapter 2

Sisters Can Be
Hazardous to
Your Health

Only Child

If you don't understand how a woman could both love her sister dearly and want to wring her neck at the same time, then you were probably an only child.

—LINDA SUNSHINE

How to Torture Your Sister

Delia Ephron

She ate her jelly doughnut at lunch.

You saved yours. It is now two hours later.

Sit down next to your sister on the couch. Put the jelly doughnut on a napkin in your lap. Leave it, untouched, until she asks you if you still want it. Then begin eating. "Mmmmmmmmmmm. This is soooooooooo good." Take a large bite and chew with mouth open so she gets a good view. Swallow and run tongue over lips. "Mmmmmmmmm." Stick tongue in jelly center and wave it around in the air before pulling it back in mouth. "Don't you wish you had some?" Take tiny bites. Lick fingers in between. "Boy—there's nothing like having a jelly doughnut in the middle of the afternoon!" Pop last bite in mouth and pat stomach.

Wander into the room when she calls a friend on the telephone.

Pick up a book and sit down on the couch. Pretend to read. Then mimic her as she begins her telephone conversation.

Hi, how are you?

Hi, how are you.

Wha'd you do today?

Wha'd you do today?

What? Wait a minute, my sister's driving me crazy. Would you cut it out.

Would you cut it out.

You dirty creep.

You dirty creep.

Stop repeating me!

Stop repeating me!

I'll kill you if you don't stop!

I'll kill you if you don't stop!

I said STOP!

I said STOP!

STOP IT!!!

STOP IT!!!

Put down book and run.

She is eating peanuts.

Whisper in her ear, "You can turn into an elephant if you eat too many peanuts. I read it in the *World Book*."

Pretend to eat shaving cream.

"Mmmmmmmmmmm. This ice cream is sooooooo good. Wanna try some?"

Follow her everywhere.

Imitate her best friend talking.

Say that her best friend is fat.

Talk to your mother while your sister is listening.

"Do you remember Christmas when I was three years old, and you gave me that stuffed animal? That was so much fun."

Turn to your sister: "You weren't alive."

You are in bed with the flu, watching television.

She has been told to keep out of your room so that she doesn't catch it, too. As she walks by the door, stare goggle-eyed at the TV:

"Oh my goodness! That's incredible! I've never seen anything like it in my life! I can't believe it! Wait till I tell the kids at school."

Do not remove eyes from set, staring in amazement.

"I wouldn't miss this for anything! I really don't believe it."

Look at your sister.

"What?"

Move over on the bed.

"Of course there's room for you."

Check hallway to see if coast is clear.

Pull her into your room, close door, put finger to lips, and speak in conspiratorial voice: "I've got to tell you something. You're adopted! No kidding! Honest. Dad showed me the papers." Pause, scrutinizing her face. "You know, now that I look at you, I can tell. You really do look different from the rest of us. I mean, didn't you suspect it yourself? Dad even knows who your real parents are—they live in New Jersey—but he said he's not going to tell you anything until you're older. He swore me to secrecy. I'm just telling you because I think you ought to know, but if you tell him I told you, I'll kill you."

You are eating Jell-O.

She is sitting next to you at the table:

"By the way, did you know that Jell-O's alive? Seriously. See how it wiggles?" Jiggle bowl. "I'm telling the truth, I really am. Lookit, you've heard of jellyfish, haven't you? Need I say more? Jell-O's like jellyfish, only you eat it." Move bowl very close to sister and jiggle again. "If it doesn't eat you first—"

She is watching television.

You are watching her:

"It's too bad about your lower lip. You've noticed, haven't you? You're kidding. Come here, I'll show you." Take her into the bathroom and place her squarely in front of the mirror. "See? It's amazing, isn't it—your lower lip looks exactly like a frankfurter. I can't believe you've never noticed. It's so obvious." Shake head despairingly. "Your looks would be just perfect otherwise. Here, I'll show you. Put one finger at each end of her bottom lip and push down. "There! Now you're normal!"

The lights are out.

The two of you are lying in your beds.

"There's an invisible man who lives under your bed. If you did anything wrong today, he'll get you in the middle of the night. Oh yes you did! Don't you remember that thing Mom got mad at you for? Good night."

My Sister's Handiwork

Bonnie Afman Emmorey

Critically Caucasian. That's what they called me. My husband and I were on a missions trip to the Dominican Republic when that title was first applied by others on our work team. I did look anemic compared to the rest of the population. Somehow the description stuck, even after our return home.

To me it seemed unfair that others around me, even my own family members, could get a tan—and I just burned. I had inherited my grandmother's skin and it did *not* like the sun. My sister Jennie had inherited skin that not only tanned well but simply glowed at every stage in the process. With our completely Dutch ancestry, how could two sisters have such opposite skin?

One summer I made a concerted effort to get a tan like Jennie's. I threw caution and cover-ups to the wind and went boating with my husband and a friend. The payback was second-degree burns covering every inch of exposed skin. The doctor was horrified when he saw me in his office the next day. He actually asked if he could take pictures for a medical journal. "They're never going to *believe* this!" he told me. That day I learned to be very cautious with my skin. No more tanning for me. I had learned my lesson.

Over the years, Jennie and I have spent a lot of time at the beach together. My family lived an hour and a half away from where her family vacationed. We would drive over for a day trip a couple of times each summer. Of course, Jennie would bask in the sun, enhancing her already luscious tan, and I would huddle under the nearest tree, shrub, or umbrella, trying not to expose my flesh.

The backs of my legs were carrying visible proof of the power of sunscreen!

Jennie would always try to entice me out into the sun, encouraging me to get "just a little." She assured me that it would make me look healthier and less anemic. Since I have been asked if I am an albino, it *was* tempting. But then I would remember my horrible burn, and sanity would return. "No, umm, no, no, I'm really *enjoying* this shady bush." I looked with longing at the rest of the world out playing with reckless abandon in the sunshine.

Then one summer, concerned about all the fun I was missing, I decided to give the sun another chance. Armed with superpowerful sunscreen purchased for the occasion, I carefully and completely covered every inch of the front half of my body. Then I flipped over and tossed the sunscreen to

Jennie. "Could you help me out? Cream my legs and back? I *don't* want to get burned!"

"Oh, Bonnie, you will look *great* with a little color," Jennie replied. But she agreed to the task.

That day we had great fun talking, laughing, and enjoying our time together. Confident I was protected, I stayed out in the sun longer than any other time. What I didn't know was how *little* Jennie actually applied as she lightly glazed her hands over my back and legs.

That evening we changed out of our bathing suits and into shorts so we could walk into town for ice cream. The kids ran ahead. Jennie and I came next, and our husbands brought up the rear. Our husbands' laughter caused us to turn around and ask what was so funny.

My husband, Ron, hesitantly said, "Honey, are you aware you have white *handprints* on the back of your legs?" Graydon, Jennie's husband, was nodding and laughing.

"What?" I craned my head around, trying to see the backs of my legs without any assistance from a mirror. "Jennie, what are they talking about?"

When I looked up and saw the look on Jennie's face, I knew it was true.

"Oh, Bonnie, I just tried to apply a light coating of sunscreen so you could get a bit more tan. It looks like I might have missed certain areas. Actually, it appears I missed quite a bit."

The backs of my legs were carrying visible proof of the power of sunscreen! It was where Jennie's hands landed with more force that the sunscreen actually "took." My sister's handiwork was clear.

I chose to give up shorts for the rest of our visit. That apparel wasn't worth the laughter it caused. And once the handprints finally disappeared, I laughed myself. What Jennie did certainly left a mark—but it wasn't permanent. I pray the imprint of Christ on my life is permanent and as visible to those who observe me as my sister's handprints were to our husbands on that hot summer evening.

You Go First

Karen Scalf Linamen

I'm a firm believer in the old adage that once you've seen someone in diapers, you get to boss them around from then on.

What? You've never heard that saying? I'm not surprised. Growing up, my sisters weren't familiar with it either until they heard it from me. As the oldest kid in our family, I can't begin to tell you the advantage I was afforded by this little piece of folk wisdom. I'm so glad I made it up.

Being the firstborn has had other rewards as well. Like the time my sister Renee and I got bunk beds. Being two years older, I got to sleep on the top bunk, which came in *really* handy the night I got an urge to scare my seven-year-old sister half to death. After our mom turned out the lights, I asked Renee if she'd like to hear a story. I proceeded to tell her an elaborate tale about an undetected nest of giant black widow spiders in an attic above a bedroom where two little girls slept in a bunk bed. After swarming into the room through a vent and killing the older sister in the top bunk, the giant spiders lowered themselves on webs to the bottom bunk so they could feast on the unsuspecting younger sister.

Shortly after finishing my story—while Renee cowered under her blanket and tried in vain to fall asleep—I tied my navy blue sweater into a gangly knot, gripped one sleeve in my teeth, and draped my shoulders and arms limply over the side of my bunk.

I hung there silent for what seemed like hours until Renee happened to uncover her face long enough to spot my dangling arms and the spidery dark shape suspended between them.

If you happened to be keeping a journal in the fall of 1969, go back and see if you were awakened one night by a bloodcurdling scream.

If you happened to be keeping a journal in the fall of 1969, go back and see if you were awakened one night by a bloodcurdling scream. It doesn't matter what part of the country you were living in at the time. In fact, I think NASA still has records of the occurrence. Naturally my parents came running. From the way they acted, I thought Renee was about to get a promotion, moving up the birth-order ladder to fill a recently vacated position of family firstborn.

As it turned out, I lived to tell the story. I also lived to enjoy my firstborn status at the expense of my youngest sister, Michelle. Trust me when I tell you that having five years on Michelle paid off handsomely when it came time to teach her the ancient Siamese proverb "Owa Tagoo Siam." She recited it for days before

Renee had mercy on her and told her to stop calling herself a goose. And you can't imagine how crazy an unscrupulous sibling can drive a younger sister by not revealing the secret to "Mares eat oats and lambs eat oats and little kids eat ivy."

These days, my sisters aren't kids anymore. This has impacted my life in ways that, unless you are a firstborn yourself, you may never fully appreciate.

For example, when we go places in the car, I'm no longer guaranteed the front seat.

I haven't gotten Michelle to recite "Owa Tagoo Siam" in years.

The last time I tried to frighten Renee with a wadded-up sweater, this mother of three boys scoffed at me and said, "*Puhlease!* There are semester-old gym socks in my laundry room even as we speak. You're going to have to do better than *that*."

As far as I'm concerned, being the firstborn has definitely lost its appeal. Not only have my sisters figured out that my diaper adage was made up, as of this moment I'm the first of us with Rogaine in my bathroom and reading glasses in my purse.

And it's only going to get worse from here.

By my calculations, I'm going to enter my second childhood a good two years before Renee and five years before Michelle. That means I'll be the youngest sister for two years and middle sister for five before things in my universe right themselves again.

I'm hoping I'm the only one who has done the math, hoping my sisters have yet to realize the *Twilight Zone* opportunity headed their way. But I'm not so sure anymore. It's possible they realize more than I think they do. Last week they started telling me that, according to all the latest research, once you've seen someone in Depends, you get to boss them around from then on.

Case of the Clandestine Carving

Patti Maguire Armstrong

My sister was a child genius! Though I was older, Mariann always emerged unscathed from every disagreement—of which there were many—while I suffered the indignity of it all and often even parental punishment.

As the oldest, I wasn't allowed to hit Mariann. Doing so would bring the wrath of Mom down on my head. Mariann knew this, and she was clever. She would find ways to bait me and then watch me squirm. When I'd reach my boiling point, she'd say, "Careful. You're about to get yourself in trouble!" Yes indeed, Mariann was one smart cookie!

Rather early on, my sister actually developed a special technique to use in our power struggle. Whenever I angered her, she would stick her pointing finger about four inches from my face and just hold it there. If I moved, she moved with me, saying nothing, and making sure there was never any contact of any

kind. The little terror knew this would be critical for her defense when I finally snapped and we were called before the court of Mom and Dad.

Mariann was a genius, but I was *no* dummy. I knew I was a victim of my own lack of self-control. If only I could outlast her, Mariann would lose interest, I reasoned. But that turned out to be an impossible task. For a while, I tried giving her a dose of her own medicine. When she pointed her finger in my face, I pointed mine back at her. We'd dance around the room, fingers inches from each other's faces, but my sister's patience and commitment always surpassed mine. I would always give up or strike out—neither good!

Mariann's maniacal behavior would have been obvious had my parents read any of the popular psychology books of the day. Instead, they espoused the philosophy that sibling rivalry is normal, and saw it as their duty to balance the scales by giving the younger, "more vulnerable," daughter the benefit of the doubt. I knew if things were going to change, I was on my own. I had to find a way to outsmart the kid, which led to an interesting observation and the formation of a devious plot.

When Mariann was not pointing her finger at someone (our sister and three brothers occasionally got fingers in their faces), she had a penchant for writing her name on things. As an aspiring archaeologist, she had an appreciation for the written clues from past civilizations that were unearthed at modern excavations. Our parents were always finding Mariann's name scribbled on walls and even clothing. It seemed to be the only thing they were willing to call her to task for.

One morning, I took a sharp object and carved "Mariann is good" on her dresser drawer and stood back to admire my work.

I felt that Mom and Dad would have no problem believing Mariann had once again been overcome by her archaeological passion—and if they doubted for a moment, I'd thrown in a backward "g" just to lock in the frame. It would be an "open and shut" case.

My actions quickly hit the fan. By that afternoon, all six of us were sitting in the living room, being grilled by our parents. *How could you guys suspect anyone but Mariann?* I wondered. *This has the little carver's name written all over it.*

But my parents were playing all their cards. Until they had a full confession from the perpetrator, no one would be going to see *Snow White* at the theater as planned. The stakes were high, but I had no intention of confessing. The word *lying* never entered my thoughts. In my mind it was a matter of justice—better late than never!

The stakes were high, but I had no intention of confessing.

Family court was at a standstill. I wasn't going to crack, and Mariann wasn't about to confess to something she didn't do. As both judge and jury, our beleaguered parents finally decided to rule in spite of the absence of a confession. "Guilt beyond a reasonable doubt" would have to be enough. Mariann was found guilty and her sentence carried out. Ouch!

My tenuous relationship with Mariann actually eased up as we grew older. As adults, we are close. In fact, my sibling rival is the godmother of one of my sons. One day, she told me her version of the infamous Case of the Clandestine Carver.

It seems Mariann had already abandoned the practice of marking things with her name for the benefit of future generations. Who knew? In her words, "Anyone who had bothered to look at the clues would have known the truth. I would never have written 'Mariann is good.' What kind of clue is that for explorers uncovering the hidden relics of the 1960s? The proper notation would have been 'Mariann was here.'"

What can I say, my sister's a genius!

Inner Sanctum

Karen R. Kilby

"It's time to go to bed, Karen," Mother said as she beckoned me to come and give her a good-night hug and kiss.

I put down my Wonder Woman comic book and looked out the window, where the night had already blackened the sky. I didn't like the dark, and I knew when I turned out the lights in my room it too would be pitch black. I wanted to stay right where I was, secure in the warmth of my family and the lamplight that chased away the shadows.

Reluctantly, I dragged my slippered feet down the hallway, flipping on all the light switches as I made my way toward the bedroom I shared with my sister, Kate. As I reached the bedroom door, I quickly flicked on the light and peered into every corner of the room. Slowly I crept toward the double bed—the beginning of my nightly custom—and cautiously peeked underneath. *Nothing there but a few dust bunnies*, I reassured myself. Pulling up

and moving to the closet, I pushed the hanging garments back to reveal the built-in drawers. *Anything or anyone could be hiding in there*, I thought. It was finally—kind of—safe to climb into bed.

Snuggling down into the covers, I waited for Kate to join me. Being four years older, she had the privilege of staying up later, but I could not close my eyes and fall asleep until I had her lying next to me—half sister, half personal bodyguard.

"Are you asleep yet, Karen?" Kate asked as she turned out the light and slid into bed. "I'm glad you're awake 'cause it's almost time for our favorite radio program—*Inner Sanctum!*"

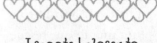

My hand clutched my pajamas around my heart. I hated that program, and Kate knew it! It scared me to death!

I scooted closer to Kate. She giggled as I trembled.

I always wished I could be brave like Kate. She has never been afraid of anything or anyone. On the night before Halloween, she led the group of brazen pranksters who went around the neighborhood soaping windows and ringing doorbells. She was well respected for her ability to stand up to bullies on the playground and in the alley on the way home. They didn't mess with Kate, and by the power of association, they didn't mess with me! Kate wasn't afraid of the dark either. In my mind, Kate was a Wonder Woman like the heroine of my favorite comic book.

"It's okay, Karen. I'll protect you," she whispered as she tuned the radio to a low volume. "If we lie real still, we can hear it without disturbing Mother."

As the eerie, creaking door of the *Inner Sanctum* program began, I scooted closer to Kate. She giggled as I trembled.

Then suddenly, Kate said in a voice only slightly above a whisper, "Uh, Karen—what's that in the corner?"

"What's what?!" I said, barely daring to move my eyes.

"Right there!" she answered. "Don't you see that tall shadow in the corner with its head hanging over to one side? It looks like a ghost to me!"

That's all it took. I shrieked as I threw my arms and legs around my sister. "Kate, Kate! Don't let it get me!"

Suddenly, the bed began to shake! I put my hand over my mouth to muffle my screams. Then I heard it—a howl like nothing I had ever heard before! Even Mother heard it!

Running to our rescue, Mother threw on the light and began to shake her head as my sister rolled on the bed in fits of laughter, pointing to the ghostly floor lamp with the lopsided lampshade in the corner of the room.

"Now, Kate," Mother scolded. "What have I told you about scaring your sister? Now turn that radio off and get to sleep!"

Ghost or no ghost, I clung to Kate that night. Every few minutes she'd begin to giggle, and after a while, I started to giggle too. Wrapping her arms around me, Kate said, "If there really was a ghost, Karen, I'd protect you. What are big sisters for anyway?"

I Was Once an Only Child

Rebecca Currington

You wouldn't know it by looking at me now, but I was once an only child. Pampered, adored, and completely secure, my parents treated me like the little princess I was. Even though the light dimmed in my kingdom when the interloper arrived, six months after my third birthday, I still recall those wonderful years when I was awarded—by reason of my very existence—all manner of attention and privileges.

I distinctly remember standing on the front seat of our car, one arm slung over my daddy's shoulder as he drove through town. These days, this behavior could buy you a child-endangerment charge and an unpleasant visit with a court-appointed social worker, but back then it signified a deep bond between parent and child. "How about an ice cream cone, my little angel?" I recall Daddy saying, as he flashed me one of his brilliant smiles.

Though money was tight, it was obvious that my happiness was all that really mattered to him.

I also have a wonderful memory of Mommy and Daddy bringing home half a dozen soon-to-be-hatched baby chicks. It seems they wanted to impart the amazing story of life to their precious darling. My parents looked on with hearts full of love for me as I clapped my little hands in excitement. Their eyes never left my face as the eggs cracked and I cheered the little yellow chickies' entrance into the world.

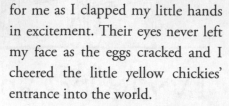
When I saw her—my parent's *new* darling—I noted immediately that she was much larger than a baby chick.

I could go on and on about the idyllic life I led as an *only* child. I could tell you about the day my mommy and I were window-shopping and saw a beautiful gray fur coat with pink collar, matching mittens, and hat in a department store window. My parents paid the better part of a week's salary for the privilege of dressing me in such luxury.

A few weeks later, Daddy brought home my first puppy, an adorable border collie I named Jeff.

Ah . . . life was good. Then—without warning—my days as an only child were over!

Of course, there had been *some* warning—my mother's protruding abdomen and unusual fashion choices, for example—but I was far too young to see these things as a prelude to another chapter of the "amazing story of life."

All I know is one day in May, my grandmother appeared and my mommy disappeared. A weird white basket on wheels

appeared in my parent's bedroom. And dinner was late. I was clueless, but what three-year-old wouldn't be?

That day everything changed for me. We sat down to dinner and Grandmother prayed—not for me, but for the precious new baby girl who had been born into our family.

Excuse me?

Then for the first time *ever* I learned what it was like to sit at the table without being the center of attention. In response, I swallowed a fish bone, which, in spite of Grandmother's careful inspection of my small portion of perch, lodged soundly in my throat. I only remember that things in the room looked strangely distorted, voices seemed far away, and finally, everything went black. Daddy told me later that I "passed out." Only my grandmother's quick action—she jammed her finger down my throat—saved me from certain death. I will always see that near tragedy as an omen, a crude premonition that life was about to throw me a curve.

When I saw her—my parent's *new* darling—I noted immediately that she was much larger than a baby chick. She also made more noise when she was awake. Most of the time, she slept in the white basket with wheels. I wasn't allowed to hold her at first. She had contracted a nasty case of impetigo, which had raced through the maternity ward like a flash fire. Though she was no longer contagious, Mommy kept her all slathered up with calamine lotion. Sometimes I would stretch up on my tippy-toes and peek over the side of the basket. Her dancing eyes would look my way, and I would think—just for a moment—that she might even be worth keeping.

I know now that I should have been nicer to my little sister. I

suppose losing my seat of power and privilege did more damage to my tender psyche than anyone realized. My sister was barely in elementary school when she began to exhibit the characteristics of arachnophobia (though her terror was hardly limited to spiders). I'm afraid I also capitalized on her fear of contracting leprosy (probably the result of hearing certain Bible stories a few too many times). In my immaturity, I couldn't help but see these fears as fodder for torture and blackmail, a way to get even with the interloper.

"Scratch my back, and I'll make sure there aren't any *spiders* under the bed," I'd tell her. "You might want to let Mom take a look at those freaky white spots on your back," I'd warn.

A more loving, more noble older sibling might have looked with compassion upon her sister's foibles, but my black heart was not so inclined.

As adults, my sister and I have made our peace. I tell everyone she's terrific, and she seems to have found it in her heart to forgive. Perhaps she felt partially vindicated a few years back when she told my boss and a co-worker that she was proud to see I now wear shoes and underwear.

Touché.

Chapter 3

Sisters Are the Perfect Accessory for Life

In a Blonde Vacuum

A blonde was playing Trivial Pursuit one night. It was her turn. She rolled the dice and landed on Science and Nature.

Her question was:

"If you are in a vacuum and someone calls your name, can you hear it?"

She thought for a time and then asked, "Is it on or off?"

—AUTHOR UNKNOWN

The Benefits of Having Blonde Sisters

Carol Kent

A couple of years ago, I was speaking at an arena event and realized for the first time in several years, all four of my sisters and my mother would be in the audience. Since I was speaking at a keynote session in front of about six thousand women, I thought it would add variety to the program to have my sisters and my mother on the platform during part of my presentation. I asked each of my sisters to share one thing they learned from our mother that they would pass on to the next generation.

Each sister's response was a tender reminder of our mother's major impact on our lives during our formative years:

Jennie thanked Mother for being a remarkable storyteller.

Paula was grateful that Mother helped her make it through a painful divorce, reminding her that Jesus would never leave her.

Bonnie reminded us that we often saw our mother on her knees and heard her praying out loud for us when we came down the big open staircase in the early-morning hours.

Joy acknowledged that Mother helped her make it through a challenging time in her marriage.

I told the crowd it was my mother who led me to personal faith in Christ when I was only five years old.

As I looked at my four sisters all standing in a row, it suddenly occurred to me that Jennie was a dark brunette. Paula was a very "highlighted" sunny blonde. Bonnie (a former brunette) was a platinum blonde. Joy's tresses were light brown, and my hair was a vibrant red.

Strong men immediately help us place our heavy luggage in the overhead compartments on airplanes.

We had all shared serious thoughts, but I thought it was time for a little levity. Scanning the crowd, I said, "I'm sure some of you are wondering how the five of us could have come from the same mother with all these varying shades of color in our hair."

The crowd murmured, and I could hear an audible chuckle. I continued, "Just so you know, except for our mother and my youngest sister, Joy, each of these colors is available to you!" The crowd exploded with laughter.

I (the redhead) will be quick to admit that when I am with either of "the blonde sisters," I always notice they get more attention than I do. When I was younger, I may have been a little jealous, but at this stage of my life, the benefits of having blonde

sisters definitely outweigh the negatives. Here are a few reasons why I like hanging out with the blonde sisters:

- We get the best seats in restaurants.

- Strong men immediately help us place our heavy luggage in the overhead compartments on airplanes.

- No one expects us to know the directions to our final destination.

- I don't have the pressure of being the center of attention.

- Other women do not find the nonblonde sisters intimidating.

- I have the privilege of helping people understand that my blonde sisters are actually highly intelligent—which makes me feel extremely valuable!

My four sisters and I are trying to act like mature adults now, but our hair colors are still available to you. We figure part of the fun of life is to keep people guessing which of us is the oldest, and we plan to delay "the graying of America" as long as can hold out.

Since "blondes have more fun," we all plan to end up in the same retirement village someday. However, the main reason we'd like to be together is the bond of sisterhood that connects us at the heart level. We have shared laughter, tears, family crises, graduations, weddings, birthdays, and funerals. And we know that being sisters has strengthened us in a way that goes much deeper than visible "roots."

Note to Self

Marti Attoun

For three weeks my sister, Winnie, dangled her bare wrist under her husband's eyes as she hinted for a diamond tennis bracelet for her upcoming birthday.

"I don't have the foggiest notion what that is," Dan finally told her. He hadn't been near a jewelry counter since buying that fob for his pocket watch in 1963.

"Oh, for heaven's sake, just do a little research," prompted Winnie. "You're always on the Internet anyway."

As anyone who surfs the Web knows, you don't do "just a little" research. One site leads to another as you follow the trail of something interesting and, three days later, you've meandered miles from base camp and are hopelessly lost.

Dan typed "diamond tennis bracelet" into the search engine and up popped a dazzling $29,000 12-carat bracelet worn by

Serena Williams at the U.S. Open. The House of Winston, jeweler to the stars, sold it.

"I wouldn't pay that for a whole tennis court," he sputtered. Walmart.com appeared next on the screen and offered its "always low prices always" version for $93.66.

If he had stopped right there and clicked on the shopping cart, then Winnie might be sporting a faux-diamond tennis bracelet today, but it was too late. He'd already closed that screen and become fascinated by another site featuring a "diamond" tennis bracelet pattern woven from seeds and beads in an ancient Potawatomi weave.

Always a history nut, he ventured into the Potawatomi Nation's site and learned more about bingo and slot machines than any human needs to know. Next up was Potawatomi State Park in Sturgeon Bay, Wisconsin, with notices about ice fishing for walleye and skiing by candlelight.

The "facts about wild turkeys" caught his attention, and he educated himself on where to look for a turkey's snood, wattle, and caruncle. If he'd even stopped right there, my sister might be wearing a diamond tennis bracelet today. The description of the turkey's bronze wings might have reminded him of his wife's bronze and naked wrist.

Too late he sidled over and clicked on the description of the park's camping sites because he might find himself in Sturgeon Bay in the middle of the night and not have money for a motel because he just lost it all at bingo. Besides, he hadn't camped out in years and longed for an outing.

But, first, Dan needed a tent. Who would have dreamed that tents now came with inflatable poles to replace the old aluminum ones? He whiled away two hours researching these trendy tents and virtually shopping for poles that could be inflated in under sixty seconds and in the dark. The self-installing tent was a beauty. Just what he needed.

Even better, his wife's birthday was nearly here, and he needed to buy her a little surprise. Winnie kept sticking her arm in his face and asking for something, but he couldn't remember what. Maybe she was waving good-bye. She needed a little getaway.

Winnie kept sticking her arm in his face and asking for something, but he couldn't remember what.

"Surprise," he told her. "I did some research, just as you said, and found it." He handed her the tent with inflatable poles.

What happened after that is known only to my sister and her beloved husband. When she shared this story with me in her high-pitched, homicidal voice, she broke down at this crucial point and couldn't go on! Little doubt, it was not pretty, but her angst was not wasted. Right then and there, I said to myself, *Note to self: Men cannot be trusted to take a hint!* I'm gonna be tucking this little piece of information away. Why should I learn such a lesson the hard way when I can watch my sister suffer and we can both be wiser!

She Had Me and She Knew It!

Tina Krause

"Pamper yourself," the salon ad read, boasting all the latest perks from pedicures to oil-scented massages. "Wouldn't that be fun?" my sister-in-law said with a glint in her eye. "Let's schedule a day to pamper ourselves."

Jackie and I are as close as sisters, but total opposites. Although we share a lot of common interests, Jackie likes to step outside the box and try new things, while I'd prefer to curl up inside and close the lid.

"Forgive me, but I don't get it," I said, shaking my head.

"Get what?"

"The whole *salon* scene. To me, pamper and pedicure go together as well as pineapple and pickles."

She leveled a clueless look, so I passionately clarified. "An invitation to sit in a shoe-shine position sipping lemon water while a stranger files my calluses and clips and polishes my toenails, is

about as relaxing to me as reclining in a dentist's chair for a root canal. I don't like people patting my paws!"

Now she shook her head, so I kept talking. "And the image of lying on my tummy while a masseuse kneads my back like a lump of stretched-out dough is, well, not pretty."

Like Jackie, other female family members have tried to persuade me about the soothing benefits of these so-called indulgences. But I am a person of a different pamper. (Ahem, and I don't mean the baby diaper variety.)

My definition of pampering equals uninterrupted solitude. Several days alone, intrusion-free, sound inviting. No doorbells or phone calls, guaranteed. All housecleaning and laundry is done, all office work complete, and no home projects nag at me. Meals are already prepared, and I can savor doing nothing or doing something, whatever suits my whim. I could read in silence, sip a steamy mug of herbal tea (forget chilled lemon water), or sing aloud to blaring music. I could take a walk or take a nap. Scented candles would illuminate my evening in dim reflections. And I would listen to the uninterrupted silence of my surroundings and the inner nudging of my latent soul.

"You know, even Jesus encouraged his disciples to *retreat* to a *quiet* place. In other words, take a break from the hubbub," I stated with a distinctive tone of biblical authority.

Jackie volleyed a snappy response. "Yeah, yeah, right. How about don't knock it until you've tried it?"

"Okay," I said, searching for a rebuttal and coming up with zip. She had me and she knew it. "You make the appointment and I'll go," I said, choking on the last word like I had a fish bone in my throat.

Meanwhile, Jackie frothed with excitement. "Great! I'll phone

the Designer's Club and let you know. We can start with a pedicure. You're free on Fridays, right?"

I sputtered something vague, but she ignored me.

On the appointed day, we met at the salon, where an annoyingly cheerful woman greeted us and escorted us to the room with "the chairs."

"Yep," I whispered to my sister-in-law, "Just what I thought. The chairs are lined up execution style. You saw *The Godfather,* right?"

"Oh, will you quit?" she said with an increasingly annoyed tone in her voice.

"Think about it," I pushed. "Some stranger is going to be handling our naked feet. I hate people touching my feet!"

"Oh, really? How would you know?" she barked. "I'm guessing no one has ever had the guts to try touching *your* feet. Anyway, these people are paid professionals, for crying out loud!"

That thought certainly hadn't occurred to me—but she had a point. I couldn't remember anyone handling my feet since I broke a toe in third grade and Mom took me to get it x-rayed and set.

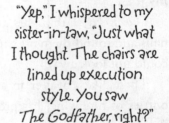

"Yep," I whispered to my sister-in-law, "Just what I thought. The chairs are lined up execution style. You saw The Godfather, right?"

Noticing I'd dropped a few steps behind her, Jackie turned and gave me the "get over here and get with the program" wave. She then exchanged niceties with everyone in the room before handing me off to a perfect stranger who asked that I take off my shoes. I grimaced.

Jackie shot me a glance as I peeled off my knee-highs and stuffed them into my shoes.

I would have shot her a look back, but I was distracted by the pedicurist, who was pouring lotion into the palm of her hand. She rubbed her hands together to allow the warm lotion to warm up her hands, and then—I'm not making this up—she lunged at my right foot.

A sound was quickly rising in my throat. I thought it might be a scream, but it emerged as an "Oh—ah" kind of thing instead. I closed my eyes as she caressed my feet with the warm lotion, stroking my ankles, toes, the top of my foot, and the bottom of my painfully high arch, before moving on to foot two.

I avoided eye contact with Jackie, afraid that my face would give away the fact that I was actually enjoying myself—just a little, anyway.

Sensing a change in the action, I looked down to see the pedicurist—named Iris—preparing huge Q-tip-like rolls on a tray near her knee. I smiled. She started placing them between my toes.

Ow, tickly, I thought, as Iris began to clip my jagged little nails and round them off with a file. I was mesmerized. I honestly could not look away.

Then, like a waiter in a fine restaurant introducing elegant bottles of fine wine, Iris presented me with three bottles of nail polish.

"All a little bright," I whispered, hoping not to embarrass her. "I'm not fond of bright colors, especially on my toenails."

I think maybe Jackie overheard because when I glanced over at her, she was rolling her eyes in my direction.

"How about one of these shades?" Iris asked, displaying three additional colors.

Finally—after the fourth or fifth offering—I selected a delicate pink.

"Perfect," she chimed, holding the bottle by the cap and banging it briskly on the palm of her hand. "This is called Cotton Candy. It's a real crowd pleaser."

I watched, intrigued, as she deftly painted the color onto my toenails. Focused with the intensity of a brain surgeon, Iris trapped the tip of her tongue between her upper and lower front teeth as she worked. One coat. Two coats, Stabilizing top coat. She finished up by producing a tiny fan about the size of the palm of her hand. It whirred away until the nails were dry.

Jackie gave me a smile and shook her head as Iris removed the rolls of cotton.

"You did it!" Jackie shouted in the parking lot.

"Yes, are you satisfied?" I replied, trying to appear pleasantly surprised rather than sheepish. I thought I'd pulled it off too, until we climbed into the car and Jackie's smile turned to laughter.

"You big baby," she said, "You loved it!"

She had me and she knew it.

The Call of the Wild, Cadillac-Style

Vicki J. Kuyper

My family has never been what you'd call "outdoorsy"—at least not since my sister and I were born. Rumor has it my parents actually went deer hunting on their honeymoon, which is even worse than it sounds when you realize that my dad's parents and extended family went along with them. My mother's first introduction to camping was cooking freshly slaughtered deer liver over an open fire for hoards of camouflage-clad relatives who hadn't showered in days. Maybe that's one reason why we never went backpacking or hiking or even had a picnic at the park as kids.

Instead, on the weekends when the weather was warm and inviting, when our family longed to get out of the house and enjoy nature, we'd take long drives in our 1960s Cadillac. Dad would get behind the wheel, Mom would slide in by his side, and my sister Cindy and I would pile in the back, where we knew the

rule was to keep quiet and not make a fuss, so Dad could enjoy his classical music and the lure of the open road.

Purple mountains' majesty, spacious skies, fruited plains—our family sampled the best America had to offer, all through the windows of our Cadillac. But we rarely went farther than we could travel in an afternoon—until the Saturday we not only made it out of the county, but across the state line.

The sun was sliding its way down toward the horizon when our long, blue Caddie turned onto an unmarked road leading into the woods. My sister and I traded "what's up?" looks. Adventure was definitely afoot.

Then the mystery deepened. Dad pulled the car off the dirt road into a clearing—and turned off the ignition. This was unprecedented. There was no restaurant in sight, we didn't need gas, and my sister and I hadn't been bouncing in our seats—the universal sign for "gotta go."

"We're here," Dad said. Where "here" was could be anybody's guess. Cindy and I anxiously hopped out of the backseat and followed Dad to the trunk of the car. To our amazement, we found it packed with "real" camping gear: two lawn chairs, a cooler, a paper bag filled with extra clothes, blankets, pillows, and a roll of toilet paper. My sister and I danced a jig of joy on the pine needles. We were going to spend the night in the wild!

The lawn chairs were set, the cooler was opened, and our dinner of cold sandwiches was laid before us. Being newbies at this whole outdoors thing, the thought of sleeping bags, s'mores, and campfires never entered our minds. But the sun was setting fast, and soon we were eating peanut butter and jelly in the dark. With the car's headlights as our lantern, our family finished up dinner

and prepared for bed. After all, what else is there to do in total darkness in the middle of some remote patch of forest?

Dad turned off the headlights and handed Cindy and me a single flashlight to help us search out a late-night pit stop. Then he popped the trunk open and told us to climb in. He and Mom would sleep inside the car. All these years Cindy and I had ridden in the backseat and never realized our Caddie could double as a tent.

Once Mom and Dad shut the door to their "room," Cindy and I bundled ourselves up in our blankets like squirming burritos. There was not a chance we were ready to settle down and close our eyes. The forest was filled with rustles, hoots, and howls.

All these years Cindy and I had ridden in the backseat and never realized our Caddie could double as a tent.

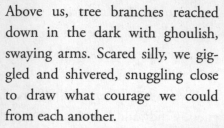

Above us, tree branches reached down in the dark with ghoulish, swaying arms. Scared silly, we giggled and shivered, snuggling close to draw what courage we could from each another.

We snapped on the flashlight and surveyed our surroundings—nothing above us but pine boughs bobbing in the wind. But below us, the forest had come alive. Drawn to the flashlight's beam was a bevy of bugs. Beetles, moths, crickets, gnats, and a centipede we would later swear was at least eight inches long, all ambled through our spotlight like pests on parade. They performed for my sister and me until the flashlight grew dim and our eyelids grew heavy.

Cindy and I awoke with the first rays of dawn, pine needles in

our hair, mosquito bites on our cheeks, and smiles still lingering on our faces. Camping was good.

It didn't take long to break camp. We climbed out of the trunk and then threw whatever was lying around back into it. I ate a few handfuls of dry cereal from the box, as I watched my dad take a swig of buttermilk out of a carton that had been in the cooler. Too bad it had curdled during the night. Our childhood farewell memory of our one and only camping trip was of Dad upchucking on a tree. You just can't make memories like that at the Hilton.

The Boy on the Sidewalk

Lynn Moore

Like most Americans during the Depression, we lived by conservative standards: Church on Sunday. No drinking. Work hard. Pay your bills. Don't waste anything. Although I was just a little girl, I understood the way things were. Because finances were tight and the world outside our door was a somber place, family time was more precious than ever. As the younger of two girls, my world revolved around our family.

My older sister, Maxene, was always fond of playing pranks.

Sometimes on Saturdays, Maxene could be persuaded to play Hide the Thimble. She loved to "hide" it in full view, just out of my reach.

"Remember not to hide that thimble on any of my salt and pepper shakers. Don't hide it on the birds either." Mother gave the same instructions each time we played. The birds were matching wall figurines just out of my reach. Of course, the figurines

were the ideal hiding place in Maxene's thinking. The thimble game was put on hold for quite a while after the time I jumped to retrieve the "hidden" thimble, only to have it and the bird figurine crash to the floor.

As we grew older, my sister started to be interested in boys, and the Saturday movies became an issue. Maxene wanted to go to the movies to meet a particular boy. Since a younger sister in tow was not part of the plan, a nickel was the price to keep me home. That was quite a bargain for Maxene, since the entire cost of the movies was thirty-five cents.

Before long, Maxene left home to serve as a nurse in the army during my junior year in high school, and our parents and I moved to a small town in southern Missouri to care for my aged grandmother. Leaving old friends and making new ones was tough. The move did have a happy ending, as I met my future husband and soon after high school would begin my own adult life. In the meantime, though, high school seemed long. Money was tight. My older sister seemed to have it all.

While I was not envious of Maxene's day-to-day encounter with serious injuries in the VA hospital, she was meeting people from all over the country. Sometimes, when she was home, she invited servicemen who were recuperating at the nearby VA hospital to visit. My mom's great cooking was a draw. My friends drooled over the number of servicemen we entertained at our dinner table.

When Maxene later moved to Colorado, it felt like my sister was a world away. Colorado! Home of mountains and snow and life lived to the fullest—great times. I remember that when Maxene came to visit, I was envious of her clothes. Although she didn't have many, the ones she had were very nice store-bought

outfits. At home we were in the squeeze of the Depression. I was still saving matching feed sacks to make a dress. Maxene had an apartment. Maxene had independence. Maxene was an adult. It was fun being her sister because I was sure that someday I would be like her.

The best part of Maxene's coming home to visit was dropping into the familiar, fun times of being sisters. It must have been a boost to Mom as well to have both of her girls home again. Our house sat right on the sidewalk, as many homes in small towns do. One day when we were cleaning the house, a nice-looking fellow walked by and caught our eyes——the dusting could wait. Maxene and I had already commented on how nice he looked. She called Mom to see. As they looked through the partially opened door, Maxene whistled and then ducked. When the boy turned to see who was admiring him, poor Mom (shocked and embarrassed) was the only "admirer" in view.

When the boy turned to see who was admiring him, poor Mom (shocked and embarrassed) was the only "admirer" in view.

I've often wondered what he thought as he looked up to see Mom staring at him from the front porch. If you know that boy (who must now be an aged grandfather himself) and have heard the story about the woman who was old enough to be his mother whistling one day as he walked down the sidewalk, tell him it wasn't her at all. It was my sister, Maxene, home from Colorado, bringing her laughter and fun back to us in Missouri.

Chapter 4

Sisters Are Born for Adventure

You Can Bank on It!

Anything you do with a sister will have her mark on it. When the family gathers and the stories are being told, she will always claim the good ideas were hers and the bonehead ideas were yours! You can go to the bank with that.

—URSULA CUMMINS

To Scheme the Impossible Scheme

Karen Scalf Linamen

There's something about sisters and schemes. During our childhood, my sisters and I peddled lemonade from our front lawn, published neighborhood newspapers, and produced elaborate theatrical extravaganzas on our back patio. One summer we secretly dug a six-foot hole in the backyard, hoping that once it was big enough our parents would *have* to agree to turn it into a swimming pool.

When you're seven, ten, and twelve, anything is possible. All you need is the right plan.

I guess some things don't change no matter what age you are.

A few years ago my sister Michelle and I were chatting at my kitchen table when suddenly she said, "Let's find a husband for Brenda."

Brenda is one of our cousins. She lives in California and is a

beautiful woman who doesn't have any trouble getting dates on her own, so I figured there had to be more to the story.

Michelle added, "Let's find her a *Colorado* husband so she'll move here and live close to us!"

Ahh! Now *that* was a brilliant scheme. Going online and visiting several dating Web sites, we spent the next two hours doing a little—what should I call it—gift shopping perhaps?

We passed up any man who began his profile with the headline, "Pick me! Pick me!" I don't care if he's quoting Donkey from *Shrek* or not. As far as I'm concerned, that kind of headline just doesn't bode well in the self-confidence department. Same goes for "Blue Light Special" and "Great Catch. No, Really."

I have to admit that "I need a housecleaner" got a second look, if only to see if he was serious.

We also skipped all the men who said they were seeking a woman who loved hiking, biking, skiing, spelunking, snorkeling, skydiving, and flyfishing *and* looked sexy rolling out of a sleeping bag at 4 a.m.

I have to admit that "I need a housecleaner" got a second look, if only to see if he was serious. This man claimed to be looking for someone who was a great cook, meticulous housekeeper, beautiful, wealthy, and financially generous. Oh, and who had a sense a humor.

"Frog in need of some kissing" was nice looking. And funny, too. But not right for Brenda. She's prone to warts.

Our search included eligible bachelors who lived near me in Denver, or an hour south in Colorado Springs, where Michelle happened to live. The exact zip code didn't matter as long as

Brenda ended up near one of us. Eventually we happened upon Mark, a handsome Colorado Springs businessman who seemed perfect. Our letter to him went something like this:

"Hi, our names are Karen and Michelle and we're sisters (and, no, your wildest fantasy has *not* just come true). We are seeking a Colorado husband for our cousin and would like to interview you for the position. Mind you, we are VERY particular and you must pass very strict standards before we introduce you to Brenda, who is, by the way, Hollywood gorgeous and a killer cook to boot (we'd tell you she has a great personality but we all know what *that* can mean). If you choose to accept this mission, let's synchronize our watches and meet Tuesday at noon at Casa Bonita on Academy. This e-mail will self-destruct in thirty seconds."

Mark actually showed up. Even better, over mango salsa and chips, he answered every one of our questions about his greatest flaws, deepest regrets, fondest memories, blood type, overdue library books, net worth, items that had been the longest in his refrigerator, how often he washed his sheets, tattoos, body piercings, *and* a catalog of his most embarrassing moments.

Before long we were sharing family photographs and swapping addresses so we could exchange Christmas cards. Mark picked up the tab for lunch, and we talked about when Brenda might fly to Colorado so they could meet. By midafternoon, the three of us hugged good-bye, agreed to talk again the next day, and walked to our separate cars. On the way to my 4Runner, Michelle pursed her lips and said, "Think it's time to tell Brenda about our plan?"

"Probably. If we wait any longer, she'll be engaged. If we tell her now, at least she can help pick out the ring."

We called Brenda that night. Honestly, the yelling and

name-calling wasn't as bad as I thought it would be. Maybe it's because we intentionally called her in the middle of the night and woke her out of a dead sleep.

The next morning she phoned Michelle and said, "I had the weirdest dream. I dreamed you and Karen arranged for me to marry some salsa dancer named Chip."

"Silly girl. The salsa and chips were just the appetizer. His name is Mark. He owns a furniture store. You're flying to Colorado Springs in three weeks to meet him."

After some arm-twisting, Brenda agreed to participate in our little scheme. Which is how, several weekends later, I found myself tossing an overnight bag in my 4Runner and driving to Colorado Springs. The plan was to meet Michelle and Brenda at a country western dance hall where Mark—who loves boot-scootin'—would be joining us. Later, Brenda and I were to spend the night at Michelle's house so the three of us could stay up until 4 a.m. eating junk food, overanalyzing every detail of the evening, and trying to get that Achy Breaky song out of our heads.

I was almost at my destination, idling at a stoplight some-where on Academy Boulevard, when I decided I needed a little freshening up. With a bottle of Arrowhead in the cup holder next to me, I was missing only a couple of items. Reaching into my overnight bag, I rummaged around until I found my toothbrush and toothpaste. Figuring a little Crest never killed anyone, my plan was to dab a little on my toothbrush, give my pearly whites the once-over, take a swig of water, rinse, and swallow. It was the perfect plan. All I had to do was remember not to spit.

Never underestimate the power of habit.

At the next three stoplights, I tried to dry the front of my jeans by cranking up the heater and contorting my body so that my lap was arched three inches from the heater vent on my dashboard.

When I finally parked and found Michelle and Brenda, I planned on playing it cool and not telling them about the oral hygiene moment in my 4Runner.

The first thing Michelle said was, "You're soaking wet. What happened to the front of your jeans?"

I sighed. "I was brushing my teeth at a stoplight and took this swig of water so I could rinse, and I should have swallowed but I spit instead."

"Oh well, it's hardly noticeable, and I'm sure they'll dry before long anyway," Michelle said doubtfully.

Brenda added, "Besides, no matter how close anyone gets, you'll be minty fresh."

The rest of the evening exceeded our expectations. Amazingly enough, Brenda and Mark hit it off and saw each other several times over the next couple months. Okay, so they didn't end up picking out curtains together, but for an extreme matchmaking stunt, I'd say it could have gone a lot worse.

Although now that I think about it, *none* of my schemes ever turn out as planned. My sisters and I didn't make millions as lemonade-stand magnates. Our neighborhood rag fell short of winning Pulitzer acclaim. The only patrons of our theatrical productions happened to be my parents. And the hole we dug in the backyard never did turn into a swimming pool, although it did make a mighty fine mud puddle. None of which seems to have dimmed the bright memories of those harebrained endeavors.

All of which makes me realize that, when it comes to sisters

and schemes—or anyone and schemes for that matter—sometimes striving for what you want *is* the main event. *Getting* what you want, well—that's nice, too, but sometimes the excitement of the journey can exceed the reward of the destination.

And speaking of journeys, an important side note: The next time you're at a stoplight and decide to brush your teeth, control yourself and look for a gas station instead.

The Great Adventures of the Tea Sisters

Susan Duke

Soon after we met and became friends, Cathy and I discovered we both loved visiting quaint tearooms. We decided we would develop our growing friendship over tea when our busy schedules allowed and seek out tearooms we'd not yet visited within a reasonable driving distance from our hometown. We dubbed ourselves the Tea Sisters, in search of the perfect tearoom—one with enchanting ambience, soothing music, and heavenly gourmet teas and tearoom fare. Once we began our drive to our preplanned destinations, we acted like two kids out for a play day.

One day after reading a newspaper ad describing a new Victorian tearoom in a nearby town, we could hardly wait to get into the car and check it out.

"I think that must be it," I suggested, spotting a newly built building just off the highway. The long winding driveway and beautiful grounds were inviting. And even though it was a metal

building, the front porch was well decorated with white rocking chairs and colorful pots of petunias and red geraniums. A lovely floral wreath adorned the door—and the fresh scent of potpourri greeted us as we walked inside.

The front room was filled with tables of beautifully handcrafted items: White and ecru Battenberg lace tablecloths and pillows, candles, potpourri, and assorted gift items. Typical for a tearoom with a gift shop, we figured.

I'm not sure, at that moment, who began howling the loudest—the dogs in the back, or Cathy and me!

"The dining room must be through those double doors," Cathy whispered. "Shall we go on in and have lunch and look around afterward?"

Before we made our way to the doors, a friendly, gray-haired, middle-aged woman bounded through them and asked enthusiastically, "May I help you?"

"We're here for lunch," I replied.

"Lunch?" she questioned, looking at me rather curiously.

"Yes, lunch," I answered. "We could hardly wait to get here. We're starving! I'm sure it will be fabulous."

The look of curiosity on her faced changed dramatically into a wide grin as she explained, "Well, unless you're starving for Kibbles 'n Bits, I'm afraid I can't help you."

I looked at Cathy. She looked at me—and we looked at the lady who had just offered us dog food for lunch. "You are kidding, right?" I asked.

"No, ma'am. I'm afraid you girls must be lost. This is a dog kennel."

I'm not sure, at that moment, who began howling the loudest—the dogs in the back, or Cathy and me! We laughed all the way to the car and all the way down the highway until we reached the area the lady at the kennels suggested we try.

This time, we knew we had found a *real* tearoom, evident from the huge sign—TEA ROOM—etched across a huge picture window. The main street of this small town looked a little run-down, but we decided whoever opened the tearoom must be someone doing their part to restore the downtown area. We were determined to have a great day, a great lunch, and some great tea!

Once inside, we observed long isles of what looked like flea market items, casually displayed on metal shelving. Not exactly what we thought a tearoom gift shop should look like! (The dog kennels had their gift room beat by a long shot!) Cathy and I looked at each other, needing no words to express, "Do you want to leave?"

She spoke up before I did.

"I don't know about you, but I'm so hungry, I'm a little shaky. Surely the food is better than the atmosphere. Let's just stay."

I agreed.

We walked to the back of the long room, where we saw several tables and chairs and a lunch counter. The menu was scribbled on an old dilapidated blackboard, and the waitress greeted us just after she excused herself from one of the tables, where she'd been sitting with several old men in overalls who were playing dominoes, chewing tobacco, and using language that wasn't exactly befitting a proper tearoom.

"You girls from around here?" she asked.

"No. This is our first time here. Is this the Tea Room?"

"Yep," the waitress chirped. "Sure is. The tea's right over there in those jugs. Just help yourself.

"Jugs?" Cathy said weakly, giving me a look.

As the waitress led us to a badly worn booth, we took a good look at the big glass tea jugs sitting on the side table—one marked Sweet and the other marked Regular.

We scooted into the booth and focused on the blackboard menu. I asked for the chicken salad and Cathy said, "Make that two."

"We're slap dab out of chicken salad, ladies, but I suppose I could whip up some 'tuner' for ya," she told us.

"Okay, then," we said in unison.

Our "tuner" special was served on dry scorched toast—spread unevenly with mustard—and a side order of broken potato chips. The tuna was straight from the can—no additives.

We smiled broadly at the waitress, who wasn't smiling back, as we slowly retrieved our purses and with a flurry of apologies— "We really have to get back on the road. We're late for an appointment . . . er . . . an auction . . . er . . . This was lovely. Thank you. Yes, thank you so much. Got to go. Long drive."—paid for our sumptuous meals and made our way out of the place.

We had no sooner cleared the big screen door then we heard one of the men say in a deep southern drawl, "Who was that?"

The waitress (proprietor, if you will) answered, "They ain't from around here."

"Didn't think so," the man answered.

On down the road, we found a Sunoco station, where we picked up lunch: Dr. Peppers and Baby Ruth bars.

No Regrets

Janice Elsheimer

When I met my sister, Norma, for a three-week artist's residency in Provence last summer, we agreed on four rules for being together:

1. No yelling at the driver.

2. No unasked-for advice.

3. Give each other plenty of space.

4. No matter what happens, *no regrets*.

These rules would all come in handy on a tour of Tuscany. But the fourth rule, "no regrets," would be the most often invoked, because we hadn't thought to add the *really* important one: Don't change plans.

It was because of a change in plans that we traveled west and then south into Spain in order to go east to Italy.

Don't ask.

It was because of another change in plans that the trip went from a six-day holiday to six days of intense anxiety. It became one of those this-will-make-a-great-story-someday kind of things.

We had just arrived at the Treviso airport when Norma suggested, "Instead of taking trains everywhere, why not *rent a car?* It won't cost much more than train tickets, and that way we won't be bound by train schedules!"

Although my usually reliable radar was flashing "Warning . . . warning," I shrugged it off and answered, "Sure. Why not?" We'd be answering that question soon enough.

Congratulating ourselves on our cleverness, we drove first to our B&B, then out to have dinner in the ancient city of Treviso. Andreas, the innkeeper, had given us his card, a map, and a key before leaving for an evening with friends. *How smart of us*, we thought, *to rent this car so we could at least go out and eat.*

Twenty minutes later, we were hopelessly lost. Andreas's map, with its 8-point-size street names and no indication of which streets were one-way, was all but useless.

"Let's see that e-mail printout with the address and phone number," I said. "We need to find out how to get home before it gets dark."

Pause. "I think I left it back in our room."

"Okay . . ." *(no yelling at the driver)* "let's call Andreas," I suggested helpfully. "You have his card, right?"

Norma held out her pinky. "No regrets?" Hungry, tired, and now lost, we'd managed to leave Andreas's card on our dresser.

No unasked-for advice, I remind myself.

"What do we do now?" asked Norma.

We managed to find the town center and the only restaurant that was open. (It was a holiday, we discovered, so the town was

practically deserted.) The owner spoke just enough English to advise us to "sit down, have something to eat, and everything will be just fine." With more gesticulation than speech, he gave us another map and directions to our B&B.

We should have returned the rental car the next morning and hightailed it to the nearest train station. Our plans had been based on train schedules, not on freeway gridlock, getting off at wrong exits, slow-moving trucks on country roads, and trying to find our way around unfamiliar cities where people didn't speak very much English and we spoke no Italian.

Hindsight. Two days and several adventures later, we arrived in Florence after six hours of driving (we'd anticipated *three*), right at sundown (of course), with no idea how to locate our hotel. All we had was an address and an assurance that it was "within sight of the Duomo." Never mind that *everything* in downtown Florence is "within sight of the Duomo"!

At midnight we parked outside a Best Western. "Very nice room for you, very cheap. Only three hundred euros," said the concierge, who offered to call our hotel for us. Rosario, Hotel Merlini's owner, came and led us to the hotel, apolo-

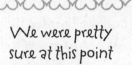

We were pretty sure at this point that renting a car hadn't been that great an idea.

gizing for the thirty euro parking fee for having the car taken to a private lot. Only after our car had been driven away did we discover that Norma left her passport, reading glasses, and one of her walking shoes in it. We were pretty sure at this point that renting a car hadn't been that great an idea.

Before leaving Florence, we made an unalterable plan: drive

straight to the airport in Treviso, get rid of the now-despised rental car, and be on time for our flight back to Spain.

Arriving with three hours to spare, though, we rethought our options: Why not "sit down and have something to eat" before heading over to the airport? What could go wrong with this one little change of plans?

"Janice?" said Norma, returning to the café from the car. "The worst thing in the world just happened."

"You broke your ankle?"

"Worse. I locked the key in the car."

Don't yell at the driver. Give each other plenty of space. No unasked-for advice . . .

Almost three hours later, having paid a locksmith forty euros (after the rental company said not to: "eet could damage the car"), we burst into the rental office, threw the keys at the clerk, and said in unison, "We found the keys!" Sprinting across the tarmac, we boarded the plane just before the door slammed.

"What have we learned?" I asked when we could breathe again.

"Don't change our plans?" Norma offered.

"No," I said, offering her a little finger. "Something more important. Whatever happens, when the sisters are together, *no regrets*."

Sloshing Sisters

Stacie Ruth Stoelting

The blonde, perky waitress smirked. She had seen us when we sloshed into the restaurant.

"Let me see 'em." She laughed. She left. Like a yellow lab, she retrieved. But she didn't retrieve our food. She retrieved people.

A group of waiters and waitresses now pooled together and stared at our table. Everyone, from the youngest teenage high school cheerleader to the older single moms to the college guys, exclaimed.

My sister, Carrie, and I smiled. We politely answered their questions.

"They're koi. They prefer to live in outdoor ponds. They can grow to be almost three feet long. And they are capable of living more than two hundred years!"

"Wow," someone said. "Let's go get John. He'd love to see this!" One striped uniform hurried into the back entrance to the

kitchen. Then the group, completely ignoring other diners, interrogated us even more.

"By the way, are you twins?" She pensively tipped her head to the side.

"Well, our mom would have been pretty amazed if we had been twins. We were born two years apart."

"Oh, wow. Well, you guys look alike. Same big eyes and light hair. Wow. I thought you were twins for sure!"

Now, John—the manager—emerged from the back.

"What's all the excitement about?" he asked.

Carrie and I looked at each other. Then we held up our gorgeous fish for his viewing.

For those of you who have not heard fish shout, it sounds like high-pitched gurgling.

"Those are gorgeous," he said, "but why did you bring them to dinner?"

The story about how we came to bring a bag of fish to dinner is quite a *fish tale*," I replied, with a smirk. "We needed koi for our pond, so Carrie and I drove out to Moesher's Garden Center to do some serious fishing. We were fortunate to snag these beautiful silver, gold, red, and orange specimens. With our catch in hand, we headed back home. But by that time, afternoon had morphed into evening—and we were hungry!"

"You weren't thinking—" We all shuddered at the thought!

"My no! We could never eat these little guys! We came here to eat your fish instead!"

Everyone clapped.

"We're not saying these beauties were crazy about our dinner invitation," I continued. "They seemed to be hyperventilating

when we first got here. After all, not many fish exit a restaurant once they enter. But we convinced them that they'd be safe with us. Now they seem content to shout out occasionally—"Where are we? Will we be going soon?" For those of you who have not heard fish shout, it sounds like high-pitched gurgling.

The dated music and slow business certainly set the stage for our table to be a sideshow. Therefore, such ingredients combined to become a most ridiculous, comically delicious concoction of waiters, sisters, and fish.

"What is your special tonight?" my hungry sister politely inquired.

"Fish and chips. Oops! Oh my gosh." The server morphed into a red koi: accordingly, she blushed and gaped.

"It's all right. I don't think they heard."

"Oh, good." She sighed with relief. We all laughed.

The fish laughed, too: How do I know? Are you kidding? I saw a burst of bubbles pop to the surface!

A Sisters' Getaway

Susan Duke

Commitments, deadlines, and stress—things we all live with daily but rarely take time to do anything about—were threatening my sanity! When my phone rang one afternoon and a perky, familiar voice on the other end of the phone said, "Pack your bags! We're planning a girls' getaway weekend," I immediately spouted all the reasons why it would be impossible for me to participate.

Two dear friends, Brenda and Marla (who are biological sisters) and who refer to me as their "adopted" sister, are the kind of friends who give a whole new meaning to the words *supportive, encouraging, merciful, forgiving,* and *funny.* To say they make me feel like family is an understatement. Despite my protestations, there was no way I was going to let them take a road trip without me!

"Oh, come on! This will be good for you! You need a break," Marla coaxed.

"You're right. I need a good extended happy hour for my soul

about now! I can be ready in five," I said, holding the phone in one hand and pulling my travel bag out of the closet with the other.

"Great!" Marla replied. "But slow yourself down. We'll pick you up tomorrow afternoon."

The plans were simple. Hotel rooms were booked in Dallas—not too far from our hometown. Travel time was a breeze—talking the entire hour it took us to arrive at our destination. We were like a bunch of kids on a field trip, primed and ready for the common adventure of just hanging out for the weekend. Snacks were packed—mostly chocolate—and we were ready to roll down the windows and throw all deadlines and other cares to the wind. We were united—with no agendas other than having fun!

The drive was everything we imagined it would be—wind whipping through our hair until we looked like escapees from an asylum. Music booming from the radio, the three of us provided a really decent backup harmony. Brenda drove, and Marla and I took turns riding shotgun. The backseat rider, dubbed Keeper of the Snacks, stayed busy taking orders and providing soft drinks, water, and other goodies for those in the front.

You would think we would have been full by the time we arrived at the hotel—but you'd be wrong. We checked into our rooms, situated our bags, and headed out for Mexican food. It was past 10 p.m. when we waddled back to our rooms and changed into our comfy, elastic-waisted pajamas. A few minutes later we had congregated in my room for chocolate desserts and the sharing of funny bedtime stories until well after midnight.

The next morning, after a hearty breakfast, we shopped, ate lunch, and spent the remainder of the day at the movies, taking coffee and ice cream breaks, forgetting we were mature women,

and playfully enjoying every moment of our sisters' getaway. By the time we were ready to head back home, our sides were aching with laughter, and we had plenty of memories.

Memories like Marla laughing so hard that she sucked in a big hunk of the chocolate bar she was polishing off. Brenda and I took turns grabbing her from behind in a futile attempt at the Heimlich maneuver. Nothing popped out, but Marla survived. As the color returned to her face, she let us know she was choking on laughter, not chocolate, and our rescue attempts had only made matters worse.

Memories like me getting locked out in the hall in my pajamas and Tigger house slippers. After letting me suffer for a few minutes as fully dressed fellow hotel occupants gave me curious looks, Marla let me in and Brenda got dressed, went to the lobby, and got a spare key to my room.

A weekend girls' getaway is to women like hunting trips are to men! Only we stay a lot cleaner and don't feel we have to cook what we shoot.

Memories like Brenda tripping over Marla's tennis shoe. After seeing that she was in for a hard landing, she attempted to launch herself onto the bed. She made it—kind of!

A weekend girls' getaway is to women like hunting and fishing trips are to men! Only we stay a lot cleaner, smell a lot better, and don't feel we have to cook what we shoot or catch on hooks or in traps! While shopping, eating out, and staying up half the night giggling would be pure torture for most men, for women—especially those who are as close as sisters—time spent together is not only one of life's extravagant pleasures, but a ceremonial bonding of hearts and spirits for life's

journey that empowers you for the tough times that are bound to come along.

Reflecting back, it was just a simple weekend—nothing extreme or wildly adventurous. No theme parks, bungee-jumping, or hiking trails. On our way home, I called my husband, Harvey, from my cell phone to say I'd be home soon.

"Did you have a good time, honey?" he asked, sounding almost sympathetic that I'd had to leave so much work on my desk.

"Of course!" I answered.

"What did you girls do?"

"Oh. . . ." I sighed, "We ate too much, stayed up too late, spent too much money, slept in, and laughed till we thought we might have to call nine-one-one."

"I'm sure you're exhausted. Maybe you should have stayed home," Harvey commented.

"Are you kidding? This is my idea of a perfect weekend!"

My Sister Made Me Do It!

Vicki J. Kuyper

The devil didn't make me do it. It was my sister. It so often is. Like the time she said, "Let's ride this piece of cardboard down that big hill!" And we did. And I ended up with a gash in my thigh that required stitches. Of course, my dad decided stitches were too expensive, so instead he administered the home remedy equivalent—duct tape. I still have the scar.

Then there was the time my sister said, "Let's put this garter snake in a coffee can and roll it down the hill!" And we did. That poor snake couldn't stop himself from slithering sideways for quite a while afterward. Unfortunately, the caterpillar she suggested we place on the cap from a cap gun—and then try to blow up with a magnifying glass aligned with the sun—did not fare as well. What can I say? My sister made me do it. So when my sister, Cindy, said, "Let's go to Churchill, Canada, to see the northern lights!" all common sense flew out the window. I not only agreed

to go, I actually thought it sounded fun. Of course, Cindy didn't mention the dogsled until later.

From a distance—say, the distance of a recliner in my family room from which I'm watching the Iditarod on TV—dogsledding looks easy. You stand behind a sled and let dogs pull you over hill and dale, kind of like waterskiing with Lassie and friends doubling as your speedboat. So when my sister and I arrived for our dogsledding adventure, and I found I got first dibs to ride in the front basket, I thought "Cool! I don't even have to stand up! This is going to be a breeze."

But "cool" and "breeze" in Churchill are something quite different from what they are back home in Phoenix. Located at the lower edge of the Hudson Bay, the average winter temperature in Churchill hovers somewhere around 25 degrees. Below zero. Not including wind chill. And today happened to be an exceptionally chilly day, several degrees below average with a clear blue sky and a razor-sharp breeze.

I thought I was prepared. I'd donned my long underwear, snow boots, gloves, and bright blue expedition suit. I resembled a Smurf ready for a sumo wrestling match, but I figured I should be warm and toasty wrapped up in the wool blanket awaiting me in the basket behind the sled dogs. And I was warm and toasty—until the dogs moved.

"Go on by!" the musher yelled. The team took off like Seabiscuit at the sound of a starter pistol. We bounced and bumped up and over frozen gullies, snow-covered tundra fields, and icy-slick rutted trails. In just a matter of minutes my fingers and toes felt like frozen fish sticks longing for a vat of boiling oil. As the snow from the dogs' racing feet and the rails of the sled hit my face like frozen BBs, I kept telling myself, "Just hold on! You get to change places with Cindy

halfway through the ride. I bet it'll be warmer when you can travel next to the musher and move around a bit!"

Optimism is seriously overrated. As Cindy and I traded places we gave each other a quick smile. (Our teeth were chattering too rapidly to carry on any intelligible conversation.) Undoubtedly each of us was convinced that now *she* had the comfy spot. But instead of sitting in a basket, I found I had to balance my two oversized snow boots, one behind the other, on a rail no wider than my thumb. Dogsledding was like waterskiing after all, only with blocks of ice for feet.

Unfortunately it wasn't just the temperature of my feet that was continuing to drop. "Oh no!" cried the musher, catching sight of my face through the fur-rimmed hood of my expedition suit. "Your nose is turning white!" The musher whisked off his glove, stuffed it into his pocket, reached into the tunnel of my hood, and pinched my nose between his fingers—as we continued to fly over the uneven frozen terrain at breakneck speed.

Now I was torn over what to be concerned about most. Would I lose my footing on the bumpy trail and fly off the back of the sled? Would I lose an appendage—be it a toe, finger, or nose, to frostbite? Would I lose my dignity by having a total stranger grip my frozen, yet running, nose for the last twenty minutes of our ride?

Luckily my dignity was the only thing to go. As we rounded the last bend into camp, the musher finally let go of my nose, which thankfully had not broken off into his hand. Later, when I relayed to my sister what had happened, she replied, "You know, you better not mention this to your husband. In the Inuit culture I think that means you're engaged."

Well, I already knew what I'd tell my husband. *My sister made me do it!*

Chapter 5

Sisters Make Good Leaning Posts

Sister on Guard!

The mildest, drowsiest sister has been known to turn tiger if her sibling is in trouble.

—CLARA ORTEGA

"Shear" Survival

Carmen Leal

Before either of my two younger sisters married, they shared a small house close to a small rural farm area in Houston, Texas. Diane preferred housework, while Patricia agreed to take over the outdoor chores. At the time, Patricia worked and attended nursing school, and usually arrived home when it was already too dark to mow the lawn. Weekends were no better, and eventually the grass grew out of control.

"Patricia, look at the yard," complained Diane. "The grass is up to my waist. When are you going to cut it?"

"It's not that bad," Patricia exclaimed.

They walked into the backyard, and while the grass failed the waist-high test, it did touch their knees.

Patricia, determined to raze the burgeoning grass before it grew unmanageable, took a day off and got started early in the morning.

It didn't take long to figure out that the lawn mower couldn't quite cut it. The long grass twisted into the mower blades with each push. Hot and frustrated, Patricia considered her dilemma: how to hack down the forest of a yard.

"What do you mean your hands hurt? How can they hurt just from using the lawn mower?"

She didn't have a sickle or weed whacker, or anything even resembling a real garden tool. At her wits' end, Patricia called Diane at her office.

"Diane, I can't do this anymore."

"Do what?"

"Cut the grass. It's too long and my hands hurt."

Confused, Diane asked, "What do you mean your hands hurt? How can they hurt just from using the lawn mower?"

Patricia, on the verge of tears, looked at her hands as she answered. "No. The grass is too high and thick. The blades won't move anymore."

"Then what are you using?"

In a small, tear-filled voice, Patricia answered.

"Scissors."

"Scissors?!"

Patricia was using sewing scissors to cut the grass. Soon blisters had formed as the scissor grips cut deeper into her flesh.

Diane tried but she couldn't stifle the urge to laugh out loud. Only Patricia, she thought, shaking her head.

"Gosh, I'm sorry, Patricia. I've never heard of anyone cutting grass with a pair of scissors."

"Well . . . I'm glad you think it's funny," Patricia moaned. "It

doesn't matter anyway. I can't do it anymore. It's going to take a miracle to cut this grass."

Later, as Diane pulled into the driveway of their small house, she was still chuckling. Rounding the corner of the house, she stopped short.

"Patricia! Get out here," yelled Diane. "You're not going to believe this."

Running outside, Patricia stared first at Diane, then at the large animal munching away in the backyard.

"Diane! Where did you get it?"

"I didn't get it. I got home and it was just here—eating the grass."

The girls gleefully laughed at their "miracle." Somehow, a hungry cow had wandered from a neighboring farm, through the broken fence, and into their yard. Everyone was happy—the cow, Diane, and especially Patricia, who had received just the miracle she needed.

Sometimes life is exactly like cutting grass with a pair of scissors—the only way to survive is with a miracle.

God's miracles come in all different shapes and sizes. Friends, family members, and seeing humor in otherwise sad situations, are just a few miracles that come our way when we need them the most.

One Day Off
Tina Krause

Pam's and Beth's busy lives made it nearly impossible to schedule a day to shop for their mom's birthday gift, especially during the holiday season.

Pam, the quintessential perfectionist, confirmed plans with her laid-back, typically-late-to-arrive sister. The plan? Meet at the mall early, so they'd have time to accomplish other errands on their only day off.

"Okay, Beth, I'll meet you at nine a.m. *Don't* be late!"

"You worry too much," Beth countered. "No sweat. I'll be there on time."

The night before their shopping date, Beth took precautions to ensure that she would meet Pam on time. She set her alarm a few hours earlier than usual to have time to jog a few miles, toss in a load of laundry, and sip a leisurely cup of coffee before leaving to meet her sister.

But a thunderstorm cut the electricity overnight, and the alarm failed to wake her. Splashing cold water on her face, she brushed her hair into a ponytail and scrambled to get dressed.

Already late, Beth made her way to the open road, but not before a school bus pulled in front of her, stopping every few blocks along the route to the mall.

"Where's my wallet?" Pam said in a panic. "My wallet! I lost my wallet!"

Forty-five minutes late, breathless, Beth scurried to meet Pam, who had already frequented two boutiques waiting for her tardy sister.

"I have *tons* to do today, Beth!" Pam chided when Beth approached her with a list of excuses why she was late.

"And I *don't* have things to do on *my* only day off?" Beth snapped.

"Let's just get shopping," Pam replied with a shrug.

The air soured with hostility, and soon the holiday shopping crowds added to their tension. Everything that could go wrong did. They disagreed on gift ideas, and when they found a mutual choice, the item was out of stock. Even after the tension cooled, their efforts to buy a birthday gift fell flatter than hair in a rainstorm.

Then the topper. "Where's my wallet?" Pam said in a panic. "My wallet! I lost my wallet!"

With Beth's calm demeanor, she reassured her sister. "Pam, let's pray and retrace our steps. We'll find it."

Quickening the pace, Pam scoured the aisles of the previous store, while Beth questioned the salesclerk. "It's behind the counter," the clerk replied. "We put it aside."

Relieved but harried, the sisters forged on past 2 p.m. and

still found no gift for their mom. Frustrated, tired, and anxious, they were ready to give up. Then, at the same moment, a store advertisement caught their eyes. It read: "One Day Only . . . Everything Off!"

"That's for sure!" both exclaimed aloud, reflecting how "off" their one day had been.

"I guess we should have shopped for God's gift of laughter first," Pam mused as she locked arms with her sister. "Yeah, and just think," Beth said, "laughter is available everywhere, costs nothing, and gives us exactly what we need the most!"

Sistership
Patsy Clairmont

Friendship is the ship the Lord often launches to keep my boat afloat. I seem to require people in my life. Scads of them. I am not the type who wants to be an island unto myself. (Unless it's Gilligan's Island.) Not that I don't want to be alone; my alone times are precious to me. I guard them and find solitude necessary for my sanity (well, what's left of it). Yet interacting with others encourages, nurtures, challenges, hones, and helps refine me. My journey has been made more joyous by connecting with friends.

One of my favorite dots in my network of friends is Carol. We are friends with history. We go back to the days when gumdrops were the latest rage in shoes. (Anyone remember those? They were a jazzed-up version of saddle shoes.)

Carol and I still tell each other secrets and giggle over our silly flaws. We know the worst about each other and choose to believe

the best. We have not always known how to do that. Then Jesus entered our lives and our friendship. He taught us important skills in esteeming one another. In our thirty-nine years of relationship, we have never not been friends; but since we met the Lord, our friendship has deepened in appreciation and affection.

We love to shop, decorate, antique, travel, dream, and scheme with each other. We have gone through the best of times in our families and the worst of times. We have celebrated and sorrowed together. We have guffawed and groaned. We have worshiped the Lord at the same church and studied the Scriptures in our homes. We have at times let the other one down, which gave us an opportunity to learn the imperative friendship skill of forgiveness.

When my wagon was draggin', Carol would catch her second wind and perform wonders in the kitchen.

Even though we share many interests, we are opposite personalities. I am boisterous; Carol is reticent. I'm a right-now person; she's an I-can-wait gal. Even physically we are opposites. She towers over my pudgy frame. Her hair is wispy and straight while mine is bushy and frizzy. Differences and similarities along with years of caring and sharing have enhanced our sistership.

Just three weeks ago I moved. I moved only seven blocks, but I still had to pick up everything and find a place to set it down in my new abode—that or have an enormous (thirty-four years' worth of stuff) yard sale. Thankfully, I had dear friends come to my rescue and help me pack.

After arriving in our new home, I was overwhelmed with the

prospect of settling in. I had thought I would pull it together rapidly. Instead, I roamed from room to room trying to remember my name. Carol came to give support (and to verify my identity) every morning for four days. She assisted me until early evening, when she would then make our dinner, serve us, and clean up. You can only guess what a gift that was to me emotionally. I never expected that kind of beyond-the-call-of-duty effort, but I'm certain our new home ownership would have found me sinking, before I could even unload the cargo, if it were not for Carol's life preserver of kindness.

What is it about moving that is so disassembling? The leaving of the old? The adjusting to the new? The disheveling of all our stuff? The initial sense of unconnectedness? Or all the above? Carol's and my long-term connectedness served as a stabilizer during this turbulent time. And it was great to have someone with similar tastes to bounce ideas off of about furniture placement, window treatments, and picture arrangements.

By evening, when my wagon was draggin', Carol would catch her second wind and perform wonders in the kitchen. This girl can cook! Every night her feast renewed our strength and our determination to get back at it. The following day we would eat the leftovers for lunch, and in the evening she would prepare yet another culinary delight.

I'm thankful that the Lord knew we would need each other to survive various storms—and that He made available the harbor of sistership.

Laughter Is the *Best* Medicine
Deena C. Bouknight

The ability to laugh—unrestrained and brightly—was passed from my mother to my younger sister and me. Our fondest memory of our mother was having her come into one of our rooms and flop down on the bed like a third sister. Before long, someone would say or do something that might not be the least bit funny to an outsider, but it incited in us giggling to the point that our bladders were strained and the tears ran down our cheeks.

We laughed with one another uninhibitedly because it tightened our bond and just plain felt good.

That laughter between us ceased temporarily when my sister, Meta, who is six years my junior, found our mother lying still on her bedroom floor. She had died suddenly and unexpectedly from an aneurism, and our smiles faded.

Shortly after her death, I decided that my traumatized sister needed a change of scenery. I was at that time a self-assured twenty-

something editor who traveled frequently to New York from North Carolina for business. I found an affordable weekend theater package for the two of us. My sister had never visited a large city, much less one of our country's most daunting. This was during the pre-Giuliani era, when New York City, though still fascinating and exhilarating, was a tad darker and more intimidating.

As soon as we stepped out of the taxi, my sister's eyes widened, and her strained appearance told me she was immediately overwhelmed. She grabbed my arm tightly and refused to let go. I paid the cabbie and struggled to maneuver my bags toward the entrance of the hotel with my sister firmly connected to me. She was looking up at the enormity of the buildings and around at the chaos of the city in a gaze of disbelief.

We came to the all-glass revolving-door entryway of the hotel. I turned to Meta warmly in hopes of calming her and told her she would have to let go of my arm for a moment so that I could get into the revolving door. She said "Okay" and let go, and I proceeded forward without further consideration. I had stepped in far enough for the door to continue moving, but it stopped abruptly. I turned, and my sister was right behind me.

We were jammed as tightly as a cork in a wine bottle. In a space barely large enough for one person, there were two of us and our bags. I tried to move forward. I asked my sister to try to back up. We couldn't budge. My sister's eyes welled with tears.

Through the glass I could see the bellhop approaching the rounder. He did not look amused or sympathetic. He looked at the unmoving door and motioned for another bellhop to assist. While they tried to figure out how they were going to get us out of the stuck door, I looked at my mortified sister and said something like, "Having fun yet?"

With that, the snickers began. Then we were both chuckling. Full-out, unashamed, obnoxious laughter soon filled the hotel lobby.

The bellhops, at this point, were struggling to move the revolving door manually a few inches backward or forward; they stared sternly at us. Like two people joined at the hip, our legs would have to move in unison—while at the same time pushing along our luggage—until an opening could be found wide enough to squeeze out our bodies and our belongings. All the while, we were uncontrollably guffawing as if we had never laughed a day in our lives and the waterfall of humorous emotions were suddenly allowed to overrun the dam.

We watched a Broadway show, ate great food, shopped, and—most importantly—we laughed and laughed and laughed.

As an exit was opened up for us and we tumbled out with our luggage, we tried to catch our breaths and thank the nice, but irritated, men as well as apologize for our foolishness. But the words only came out in half syllables in a manner hardly respectful as our laughter continued and the tears drenched our cheeks. The bellhops sighed, grabbed our bags, and plopped them down by the check-in desk. The hotel clerk was the model of professionalism as we struggled to bring our fit under control. I apologized to her for our disruption, and pulled two $10 bills out of my wallet to give to the bellhops for their trouble.

We got our keys to our rooms and walked toward the elevator. My sister had a smile on her face. "I really am sorry I followed you so close," she said as the doors opened.

"I'm not," I answered, smiling back.

I knew in that very moment the deepest meaning of the adage: "Laughter is the best medicine." My sister's laughter began the healing process in her that would continue. She still held my arm or my hand during our entire weekend in New York, but I didn't mind. We watched a Broadway show, ate great food, shopped, and—most importantly—we laughed and laughed and laughed.

Now, almost fifteen years later, we both have our own daughters. Whenever I get together with my sister and her daughter, we inevitably, at some point during our visits, plop down on the sofa or the bed with our girls. We will tickle them, make a silly face, or say something that no one else might think is funny, and soon there will be a wave of giggles that will build into a flood of laughter.

My sister and I can laugh with each other like we can with no one else in our lives—freely.

The Doctor Is Awake

Karen Scalf Linamen

I'm writing this at three-thirty in the morning.

Exactly one hour ago the cell phone on my nightstand gave three short chirps and woke me from a dead sleep. I picked it up and blinked at the display. Who was texting in the middle of the night? I guessed it was my sister, Michelle, who works nights as a dispatcher for the Colorado Springs Police Department, or my daughter, Kaitlyn, a full-time college student.

I opened the message and read the words, "U up?"

It was Michelle.

I thumbed back a "Hey" on my BlackBerry.

Michelle typed, "Were u sleeping?"

"Depends what u mean by sleeping. If you're talking about that unconscious-snoring-REM-phase thing, then sure, I guess I was sleeping. You ok?"

"Kinda down. But go back to sleep. We'll talk tomorrow."

I wrote, "Look, if it's about men, everything's going to be okay. Sure, neither one of us have men in our lives right now, but we're strong and beautiful women and we're going to be just fine. I promise and cross me heart." I glanced back at what I had just written, noticed the typo, and added, "When did I turn into a pirate?" and hit the send key.

At that very moment my phone chirped again, and lo and behold, I had a text message from Kaitlyn. I opened it up and read, "I hate my life. The coffee shop down the street charged two hundred sixty dollars on my debit card instead of two dollars sixty cents and now I've got four bounced checks and I'm supposed to call the bank and get it straightened out but I'm so overwhelmed by the whole thing I can't even make the phone call."

I wrote back, "Tomorrow we'll call together :). At moments like these, we need to get in touch with our strong inner cores and rise to the occasion and do the thing we think we cannot do, but really can."

I looked for a reply from Michelle on my pirate comment, but there was nothing. I sent her another text: "What, no response? Stop saving lives and answer me."

She keyed back, "Sorry. Just sending units rolling on an ax murderer/terrorist/sniper call. What were you saying?"

I typed, "Ax murderer? Cool! Maybe he's single! You know me—always looking for that silver lining."

By now Kaitlyn had written me back. She'd written "OK" as in "Okay, tomorrow we'll call the bank together."

I answered Kaitlyn by firing off a series of texts reminding

her that, in the middle of the night, it's easy to let fears and worries eclipse hope and reason. I encouraged her to get up in the morning, take a deep breath, detach the task at hand from any feelings of inadequacy or anxiety, and simply dial the phone and get it handled. I reminded my daughter she was a strong, capable woman who planned entire mission trips *and* kept her mother in line, and I knew she could handle this simple phone call with one hand tied behind her back, as long as it wasn't her dialing hand.

Going back to my conversation with Michelle, I added, "Speaking of silver linings, you know, our lives could be worse. I was at the tire store today with Dad and there was this clerk. I couldn't tell if it was a man or woman. When he/she asked for my license plate number, I said, 'Actually, it's on the paperwork, I gave it earlier to the guy who works here,' then cringed because if the clerk in front of me was a man, I probably should have said, 'I gave the paperwork to the *other* guy who works here.' Eventually I figured out how to solve the mystery and asked, 'What's your name?' The clerk said, 'Jess.' *Great.* Wouldn't you know he/she would go by a name like Jess? By the time I came to the conclusion that Jess was definitely a woman, she and Dad were in middle of a spirited conversation about cars. Dad said, 'I like you. You're a

There *was* a man in our lives who adored us both and would love to take us for moonlit strolls in the park, even if he did wear a rabies tag and liked to lick his own fur.

fine young man. You're going to go far in this business.' Which is why you and I need to cheer up. We don't have men in our lives, Michelle, but at least no one *thinks* we're men."

In the middle of all this texting, I wondered why psychologists and life coaches don't offer night hours. Obviously there's a huge market. I know in my own life I've had plenty of my own wakeful hours when worries seem to run amok. Wouldn't it be cool to call an 800 number and get nocturnal pep talks as needed? Then again, maybe the whole system works fine as it is. After all, while our therapists are sleeping, we get to pick up the slack and encourage each other. I know that my sister, my mom, friends, and both my kids have been there to defuse *my* sleep-deprived fears in the middle of the night. I considered myself blessed to be there for Michelle and Kaitlyn now.

Picking up my thoughts with Michelle, I assured her that there *was* a man in our lives who adored us both and would love to take us for moonlit strolls in the park, even if he did wear a rabies tag and liked to lick his own fur.

At that moment, something began to dawn on me—I hadn't gotten any messages back in a long time.

I fired off another message to Michelle. "Hey, where are you?"

She wrote back, "Can't text now. Go to bed. Luv u."

I dialed Kaitlyn's phone number. On the fourth ring she answered.

I said, "Hi! Whatcha doing?"

She said groggily, "Sleeping."

"You're *sleeping?*"

"Yeah. I went to bed. Can we talk tomorrow, Mom? I'm beat. Besides, do you realize what time it is?"

We hung up.

I blinked at the phone. After a while I went downstairs and got my laptop. Back in bed, I logged on and stared for five more minutes at a blank page and blinking curser. Eventually I typed, "I'm writing this at three-thirty in the morning."

Do I know what time it is? You bet I do. Time to start posting office hours, *that's* what time it is.

Chapter 6

Sisters Are Familiar Strangers

Family Origins

Sisters may share the same mother and father but appear to come from different families.

—AUTHOR UNKNOWN

Me Too!
Nancy Hoag

Before my sister was born, I might not have understood all that much about pregnant mothers or how they got to be so round and crabby, but I did understand mine was looking forward to this *new* baby. Which meant poor me, poor me—not even two and already the big sister—would, from now on, have to walk on eggshells around the "precious" crybaby.

By the time I'd started school, I'd already had my fill of "You can go, but take your little sister." Or "You can play dolls, but let your sister choose first." And if a real friend—someone neat and special—wanted me to come swing or feed ducks or rabbits? *She* had to tag along with us. Mom didn't have to take time from her curtain stretching or picking peas to say it, I just knew. My sister knew it too.

Then there were the visits to Santa *long* after I'd decided I no longer believed. I was told to pretend and sit on some old man's

lap and look dumb. What did it matter if *my* school chums might just happen by and giggle?

By the time I'd reached junior high, even my best friends were groaning, "Why do you always have to bring *her*?" But the very worst was her constant, daily, even hourly, "Me too!" If I wanted Grandma's jam on my toast, before I'd taken my first bite, I'd hear, "Me too!" If I wanted to skip rope or play jacks or Kick the Can with my *own* pals on our road? "Me too!" my sister would sing. Anything good enough for me would be really good for her! She'd do or eat everything based on what *I* decided, and she'd ask to have her hair cut just like mine! She even adored wearing my clothes, marched behind me in the Saturday drill team, and watched to see what I'd say or play. It seemed she was always right behind me. One time, while playing with a special friend, we ran from her, thinking she would never catch up. But she did—without losing the smile on her face. That copycat, me-too sister of mine!

If I wanted to skip rope, play Jacks, or Kick the Can with my own pals on our road? "Me too!" my sister would sing.

Eventually I married and left my little me-too sister behind. One day, I began to feel a little bit queasy—not sick, exactly, just bloated and tired.

"You're not pregnant, are you?" a colleague asked the day it became clear I was spending more time in the ladies' rest room than at my workstation.

Pregnant? I hadn't thought about the possibility; still, at my friend's suggestion, I called an OB/GYN—and sure enough, I

was expecting a baby! I couldn't believe it; I'd be doing something my sister could *not*! Well, actually, she could, but she hadn't. To be honest, I was looking forward to showing off, shopping, and putting a nursery together without her.

"Oh, wow!" I told a female colleague. "Wait till my sister hears, *and* wait till I tell *her* mother!"

We attended the same church (of course), and almost always the very same pew. Only, this Sunday, it wouldn't matter. I had something I would be telling *and* doing that she would *not* be able to copy. I hoped I'd be able to wait until after the sermon was over, hoped our pastor would keep it short. This was going to be a first. I'd be making our mother a grandmother!

When the service ended, I wended my way through the narthex (and I'll admit it, I was gloating and giving myself the applause I was sure I deserved). I'd only just made it into the fellowship hall and opened my smug mouth to proclaim, "*I'm* going to have a baby—" when my sister turned around and smiled that smile that said she liked me—even if I didn't always act like I liked her—and sang out, "Me too!"

Me too? She would also be producing a grandchild? "When?" I blurted. Surely she hadn't heard and then hurried to copy—nah!

"Mid-January," she said. "But what about you?"

What about me? My doctor had indicated it would be toward the end of January. This meant my sister would be having her baby only days before me? Maybe hours?

"Isn't this wonderful?" I heard. "We'll have babies together, and then they'll grow up and play and be such good friends! Just like you and me!"

"Just like—?" And then it hit me. My cute little sister wouldn't be the copycat this time! The tagalong to the hospital wing would

be "Fatso," me! "Special," I said, suddenly thinking maybe it hadn't been all that wonderful for her dealing with an older sister who was always trying to ditch her. "Right," I barely whispered, as we made our way to the punch and cookies. "And if we both have girls . . . ?"

My sister turned to grin.

"Don't *even* suggest!" I whooped, just like when she'd onetime hinted we ought to be singing duets. "There will be *no* matching hats and booties!" I added, as firmly as I could without laughing, my mind flooding with visions of home-sewn smocks and a two-bed ward.

"No?" she said, smiling broadly.

The Wonders of Identity Theft

Marti Attoun

Identity theft has been in the headlines a lot lately, and my sister is hoping to be the next victim. She just renewed her driver's license.

"Look at this photo. I look like I've been living in the bottom of my purse," she gasped. "If anyone wants to steal my identity, they're more than welcome to it. It's out there on the dash of that eighty-five Honda."

Worse, she'd paid extra so she wouldn't have to return for six years and get another frightening photo.

"Oh, it's not so bad," I said. "I've taken worse."

"When?" she demanded.

I couldn't lie. "Oh, you know. On that last camping trip." I didn't need to elaborate. She remembered the trip where it rained three days straight and my hair mildewed.

Really, though, this identity theft could backfire on the thief. For example, the other day the man in front of me at the supermarket

frantically scrambled for his driver's license so he could write a check. He finally pulled out a membership card from the International Dull Men's Club.

"A little gag gift from my wife," he explained to the clerk. "She claims I'm as exciting as a hubcap."

Does anyone really want to be identified with that?

"That's funny, sir," the clerk said, "but I still need to see a photo ID."

He kept poking around in his wallet and finally turned around so the clerk could read LEROY tooled in leather on the back of his belt.

"That won't do," she said. "I still need something with a photo."

Leroy thumbed his wallet some more and pulled out his tattered frequent pizza-eater card with six punches. Four more punches would earn him a free twelve-inch pizza. The poor guy shuffled his deck of cards—credit cards, library card, movie rental card, business cards, supermarket discount card, AAA card, bookstore discount card, Lions Club membership card. He got so frustrated he ended up paying with cash.

I'm not sure I'd wish my mother's identity on anyone, either. Her bundle of rubber-banded identification cards weighs a pound.

Identity theft definitely has its drawbacks for the criminal, I told Winnie.

She continued to bemoan her driver's license photo, wondering if she could request a reshoot or some photo editing. She compared it to mine, only a shade less scary. In fact, they were similar—same hairstyle, same body size, same eye color.

"Hey, wait a minute," I said, and snatched back my ID.

You can't trust your life with anybody these days.

It's Your Urn

Nancy Rue

"You're not going to believe this."

At the sound of my sister's northern-Florida drawl, which I had never developed, I looked up from the stacks of letters I was stuffing into a black trash bag. "What?"

Phyllis emerged from the linen closet she'd been dismantling and presented a stack of very old, very thin, very faded dishtowels, all ironed and folded as carefully as though they'd been Prince Charles's boxer shorts. My mouth dropped open a little bit. "You're not serious."

"Oh, I'm serious as a heart attack. Do you remember drying dishes with these?"

Unbelievably, I did. "The woman saved everything. I'm expecting to find our baby diapers any minute now."

Our mother, our Mu Mu, as we'd dubbed her years before, had been dead for a little over a week. We'd hurried down to

Fort Lauderdale to clean out the condo she hadn't lived in for more than a year. The place was, of course, as neat and orderly as everything in her life had always been. But her Depression era ethic of saving every last scrap of anything with a possible future use was not making our job easier. We had long since sent our husbands out to do . . . well, anything but stand over us and sigh impatiently. This was hard enough as it was.

Phyllis waved the stack of midcentury terry cloth at me again. "You want these?"

"Uh, I'll pass. Don't you want them?"

She examined them again, a little scowl crossing her moon-shaped face. She looked just like Mu for a few seconds. She *was* so much like her: both holding up impeccable standards for cleanliness, both great cooks, both seamstresses and craftswomen. Neither shy to tell anyone and everyone exactly what they thought in no uncertain terms. But I'd been much closer to Mu than Phyllis had, though I shared few, if any, of these qualities. I'd been—*encouraged* seemed too gentle a word—urged, perhaps, to spend my time studying and playing the piano. Seven years Phyllis's junior, it was to her I turned for female information, like what was going on with bras, and how to shave one's legs. Mu would have kept me in knee socks and smocking forever.

Phyllis was still scrutinizing the dishtowels. "Phyl?" I said.

She sighed. "I don't think she made these. I guess they're outta here." She tossed them to me, and I stuffed them into the trash bag before either of us could reconsider. My pile was already giving me waves of how-will-I-get-this-home anxiety.

Phyllis delved back into the closet, and returned with two embroidered pillowcases and a needlepoint sampler. "Mine?" she said.

"Go for it," I said.

She carried them off to her pile, a growing mass of similar

objects—the samplers, pillows, napkins, and even clothes Mu had made over the years. There had been little bickering between us about who got what. My pile, slightly smaller, were things I knew Mu had bought and cherished when she traveled—she was the daughter of a factory worker, one of twelve, and having enough extra money for knickknacks was huge to her. Mu had pushed me so hard, I knew, because she believed that only by making the most of *myself* would *I* be able to have the things I wanted in life. I looked again at my sister, who ironed perfect creases and tied perfect bows. Why had Mu expected lesser things from her?

No one could find charm in something so ugly, least of all our Better Homes and Garden mother.

I rubbed a hand over my tired, cried-out eyes and got back to the desk I was emptying. Mu, apparently, had saved every letter *anyone* had ever written her. To one side were lots of short little missives from Phyllis; to the other, fewer, but fatter, letters from me. Mu would have wanted me to look through each one, save the ones that were "important," but we'd been there all day, and I didn't have it in me. I swept them all into the bag.

"Okay, what the *heck*?" Phyllis reappeared, a look of total exasperation on her face, and one hand on her hip. In the other, she dangled a jar-shaped vase, brown, badly chipped on the side, by two fingers, as though it was full of something really appalling. "Do you remember this thing?"

"Yes!" It was like Laura Ingalls Wilder gone wrong, that thing. No one could find charm in something so ugly, least of all our *Better Homes and Gardens* mother. "I never understood it."

"I know she saved *everything*, but this is pushing it, even for

her." Suddenly, Phyllis's face took on the hard rebellion it had always worn in the fiercest of mother-daughter battles. "I am not keeping this! I am throwing this out!" She stormed to the trash bag, swinging the vase up like she was going to hurl it in there, smash it to pieces, and really let Mu have it, once and for all. That's when I saw the tape on the bottom.

"Wait!"

"What?"

I pointed, and Phyllis turned the vase over. The tape was yellowed, Mu's writing scrawled across it. We leaned in.

"This belonged to your greatgrandmother Deardon," we read in unison.

That was all it said, but Mu's voice seemed to echo it, and the weight of it settled on us. A few seconds past. Then I snorted.

"Wow," Phyllis said. "A bona fide heirloom. No wonder Mu held onto it."

"Hey—there aren't any ashes in there, right?" I asked with a touch of panic.

"Nope, it's just an ugly old vase that apparently our mother *cherished*," she responded. "And we nearly threw it away!"

Phyllis put her hand over her face and started to shake. I put my arms around her, and we laughed. And then we cried, giving release to the emotion we had been stifling all day.

After a minute, Phyllis wiped my cheeks off with the sleeve of her shirt. Then she tried to hand me the vase.

"No thanks, Phyl," I said, extending the palm of my hand.

"Well," she said, turning back to the closet, "I could take it since I'm the oldest. But I always get the good stuff. I sense Mu wants you to have this one!"

Lizard Boots and Wedding Bells

Vicki J. Kuyper

The weekend of the wedding began like a disaster movie. I boarded the plane to the sound of rumbling thunder, eyeing my fellow passengers in the eerie flashes of early morning lightning. In front of me was a woman with half her face wrapped in surgical tape. Behind me stood an adolescent boy, apparently dressed for Halloween—ten months early. Behind him walked a priest with a violin case. Each of the fifteen passengers quickly found his or her seat in the sixteen-passenger plane. The only vacancy was to my left. Seat 13. It figured.

As we taxied down the runway, the flight attendant pointed out the plane's safety features. I was amazed to find it had three emergency exits, one of which was directly above my head. I tried to calculate the force it would take to fit my size 12 hips through a size 7 exit.

In a loud burst of roaring and shaking we cleared the runway

and, with a little extra effort, the airport itself. The town below became a misty blanket of fuzzy lights in the morning drizzle. As we gained altitude, the sun appeared over thick clouds that clung tightly to the hills. The clouds had the quality of spun sugar, reminding me of circus tents, playing house, and my kid sister.

Cindy, now twenty-one, constantly ate but never gained weight, broke up with one boyfriend on Monday only to find a new "love" the next day, and had always been my best friend.

We were met by a flurry of western music, ringing, flashing slot machines, and loud bursts of laughter.

She was loud, hated school, loved horses, and swore she'd never marry a guy who was a bull rider, drove a Ford truck, or chewed tobacco. Hank was three for three.

After a surprisingly uneventful flight our toy plane touched down at the Reno airport with a lurch and a bounce, rolling in next to a 727. Our plane looked like a Matchbox car trying to fit in at the Indy 500. But we made it. We were on the ground. I was actually in Nevada to be a witness for my sister's spontaneous "saloon" wedding.

Once inside the terminal, I spotted Hank's cowboy hat through the crowd. I looked at my kid sister, clinging to his side, as much a part of him as his tin of chewing tobacco. As big sister, my "bodyguard" persona had evaluated several guys as potential brothers-in-law over the last few years. In my mind, Hank didn't measure up. But I'd talked with Cindy about my concerns, and she was convinced Hank was her "dream come true." What was a big sister to do?

As we walked through the airport parking lot, I watched Hank

spit a wad of tobacco between the rails of a fence right onto the hood of a nearby station wagon. Clint Eastwood would have been jealous of that kind of quick-draw accuracy. It was hard for me to stifle an audible sigh.

After a quick stop at the bathrooms of the Bonanza Inn to don our wedding attire, we climbed back into Hank's truck and wound our way through the tumbleweed-speckled Nevada foot-hills to Virginia City. The old Gold Rush town oozed nostalgia with its antique-filled, Old West–style buildings. Our destination was the Silver Showgirl Saloon. Not my first choice for a wedding ceremony, but, once again, I was just along for the ride. This was little sis's big day.

The click of Cindy's three-inch heels echoed loudly against the old wooden sidewalks as we made our way through the almost deserted streets of town. The ruffle of her long white dress billowed behind her like a silky cloud, gathering red dust. Hank ambled along by Cindy's side in his western-cut shirt, blue Wrangler cords, hand-tooled leather belt that announced HANK across the back, glistening silver bull-riding buckle, cowboy hat with a white foo-foo feather flowing in the breeze from its place in an Indian braid hatband, and his faithful can of chew bulging from his back pocket. Right down to the points of his lizard-tipped boots, Hank reeked of country.

Taking the lead, Hank pushed open the saloon's swinging door. We were met by a flurry of Western music, ringing, flashing slot machines, and loud bursts of laughter from near the bar. In the back of the room between two slot machines was a splintered wooden door with a sign that read: WEDDING CHAPEL. Hank and Cindy exchanged silent smiles. Then we headed toward the "chapel," passing a huge painting of a dance-hall girl. I did

a double take. Real silver dollars were glued in place to form her dress. That was a wedding motif I'd never encountered before.

But there was so much more behind the door. Half of the small room was cement, painted white, with a maze of white-painted pipes near the ceiling. The other half was covered with yellowing wallpaper on which silver cupids flew aimlessly above a silver and blue Saint Francis of Assisi holding silver birds in his outstretched silver palms. At the front of the room, a tiny niche outlined with Christmas lights surrounded yet another Saint Francis. Two rows of candles stood on either side of the niche. If you wanted the candles lit, well, that would be five bucks more.

A marriage certificate was shuffled my way. I surveyed the couple before me, each supporting the other to stand. Cindy glanced up at me with the hint of a shy smile. I turned to Hank, looking him squarely in the eye. He raised his chin and met my gaze. At that moment, a mantle was passed between us. Hank would care for my sister, love her, protect her, be her partner through joy and through pain—a job I felt had always been mine. No wonder Hank rubbed me the wrong way. No one comes between my sister and me. With a quick sign on the witness line, Cindy and I left childhood behind. It was time to discover a fresh, new season of sisterhood.

"Dearly beloved," a squat bald man shaped like a beer mug began. "Do you take this woman to be your lawfully wedded wife?"

"Yup," Hank replied.

"And do you Cindy . . ." Cindy answered the man's questions, her soft voice almost inaudible against the rhythmic *plink* of the slot machines sounding in the background. Hank held Cindy's hand firmly, yet tenderly, gently rubbing her fingertips with his own. I felt the strength of each of them reach out for the other.

Even the lizard-tipped boots and now half-empty Copenhagen can didn't seem too offensive at that moment.

Two minutes later, it was finished.

"You may kiss the bride," boomed the wrinkled-suited man.

Beneath the dusty paper bells that hung in the peeling white wooden arch intertwined with powder puff pink plastic flowers, Cindy smiled and Hank feigned gruff as I clicked off a few photos. The new Mr. and Mrs. Hank Bowman walked out into the bright flashing lights and boot-stomping beat of the saloon. They looked around anxiously, a little embarrassed at Cindy's white dress and the obviousness of it all.

Two old women, who'd undoubtedly been watching the long trail of re-newly weds with their lifted faces and false hairpieces that had been filing through the chapel all day, whispered excitedly to each other.

"Look, Berta!" one of them said to the other. "I think it's a *real* one."

Her friend nodded, grinning widely.

And you know something, I think Berta and her friend just might be right.

Not Nice—but Interesting

Patricia Mitchell

"Growing old—it's not nice," noted novelist and playwright August Strindberg, "but it's interesting." Interesting, indeed. Seven years—seven years!—separate my big sister and me, and you would think she'd be the first of us to discover the not nice, interesting aspects of growing old. But no.

"Hey, you're Janice's sister, aren't you?" exclaims Ms. Mutual Acquaintance.

"Yes, I am."

"Oh, I think so much of her," gushes Mutual. "She's such a fun person to be around! And she's my little Missy's favorite teacher!"

I nod in agreement and bask in glory by association.

"So—are you twins," probes Mutual, "or are you older than Janice?"

Not nice. Not even interesting to me, but a source of great amusement to Janice. "It's the gray hair," she says, perhaps trying

to soothe my wounded pride, but I detect her pleased expression. True, I let my hair find its natural shade after I retired from my corporate gig. Mostly I got tired of chasing dark roots, but I also took inspiration from baby boomer celebrities who have dared to go gray in their fifties and sixties. They look comfortable with themselves. At home in their bodies. "Naturally gray hair," I claim, "makes us appear confident and authentic."

"It makes us appear old," my sister says, as she dashes off to her highlighting appointment.

And here I spent my entire childhood wishing I could be as old as Janice. It started the afternoon I snooped in her closet.

"Can I have a big skirt with lots of petticoats?" I asked my mother. "Will you buy me some flats to wear to school?"

"When you're older," she said. So fluffy, starched petticoats hung in Janice's closet, not mine. A collection of cute flats lined her closet floor. My skirts hung cotton-cloth limp over a couple of pairs of oxfords while I waited to get as old as my big sister. As life would have it, by the time I reached the age where I stood a chance at wrangling petticoat permission, poodle skirts and flats had given way to miniskirts and go-go boots—which, of course, I couldn't wear until I was older. Not nice.

Janice's twenty-first birthday opened a whole array of interest-ing activities available to her—but, of course, not to me until I was older. She could date and go to nightclubs on the Sunset Strip. I had to stay home in Santa Monica—not a bad place to call home, but it's always the other person having the glamorous life, no matter where you live.

Occasionally, however, she let me glimpse firsthand the full extent of the privileges that come with age. One time, Janice and her date invited my girlfriend and me to go with them to see

the Smothers Brothers. Cooool! So what should I wear? Those
were the days when a twenty-one-year-old woman's garments
differed markedly from those appropriate for a fourteen-year-
old girl. But I don't remember what I wore (though I'm sure it
was a source of great embarrassment to me at the time). I don't
remember what my girlfriend Chris wore either. But both Chris
and I well remember Janice's little black dress. Her little strappy
heels. Her glittery earrings. "Wow," Chris and I agreed, wishing
we, too, were twenty-one.

"You're too young to wear black," my mother said the next
day when I suggested a wardrobe upgrade. "And no, you don't
need high heels like Janice's." I
vowed all that would change if I
ever—ever!—turned twenty-one.

*"You don't need high
heels like Janice's."
I vowed all that
would change if I
ever—ever!—turned
twenty-one.*

When I reached my twenty-
first birthday, the petticoat episode
played itself all over again. Prairie
smocks had supplanted little back
dresses. Birkenstocks had rendered
little strappy heels the sure sign
of an unenlightened, preliberated
woman. I allied myself with my
age group and adopted the current styles, though I passed on the
opportunity to burn my bra at a women's rally in MacArthur Park
and wear overalls and camp boots to work.

Now Janice and I live next door to each other in Kansas
City, where people who know both of us remark on our resemblance—and our "obvious" closeness in age. I'm even mistaken
for my sister, as when a former student of hers, a clerk at the
Sherwin-Williams paint store, asked me, "Aren't you Mrs. Pena?"

"No, I'm her sister."

"Oh," he said. "You look just like her."

Just give me my paint, kid.

Such encounters have spawned several conversations between us about aging. We try to keep the subject upbeat and interesting. But not-nice things are relevant, so we're planning how we're going to act when we get older—really older: We're going to stay involved. We're not going to talk about our aches and pains. We're not going to tell everyone we know that our medications are taken with (or without) food. Sort of like Chris and me sitting on the beach and swearing we'll never—never!—impose curfews or dress codes on our kids.

"Most important," Janice declared the other day, "we're going to tell each other when we need a hearing aid." She pointed her finger in my direction for emphasis. "We're not going to let each other run around hearing only half of what's going on!"

I didn't quite get everything she said, but I'm sure it was interesting.

Birthin' Babies

Becky Freeman Johnson

One might expect that in bearing children, we are all sisters under the skin, which is true. However, no two births are ever exactly alike, and my sister, Rach, and I bore children under incredibly different circumstances. When my first child, Zachary, was born in the late seventies, the watchword of the young and idealistic was "Back to Nature!" Lamaze was the only way to go. Therefore, I would give birth in the warmth and intimacy of our own home, in natural, cozy, unmedicated, excruciating pain.

My first baby was born after a twenty-eight-hour labor, and three hours of pushing, and delivered by a male ex-marine-sergeant-turned-midwife. One thing about having a marine for a labor coach is that when he barked "Push!"—no matter how exhausted I was, I wasn't about to ignore orders. After two hours of pushing, I would have cheerfully strangled every natural childbirth expert who had ever told me that labor was not really

painful, just hard work. Look, I know hard work. I was a friend of hard work. And this was no hard work. This was PAIN. But the nine-pound, two-ounce miracle that finally made his arrival was worth it all.

My second child arrived in June, and was oh so much easier. Our garden had yielded its abundance at the same time Ezekiel was born, and my mom still laughs at the memory of bathing her newborn grandson in the kitchen sink alongside five bushels of zucchini, organic, of course. While I was Earth Mother personified, Zeke was the original Cabbage Patch kid.

Baby number three, however, would have none of making her appearance on a warm summer morning. Rachel Praise made her debut three days after Christmas in 1982, one of the coldest winters in the history of Texas. My parents and my sister, Rachel, eighteen at the time, were visiting for the holidays, and they all needed to return home. I was overdue and felt like a watched pot waiting to boil. Finally, at about two in the morning on December 28, I woke my husband to tell him I was in labor.

"Go back to sleep," my young husband, Scott, yawned. "I don't even think you're pregnant anymore."

The interesting thing is, I managed to do it, but when I next woke up there was absolutely no doubt. The baby's head had crowned. I was pregnant, but I wouldn't be for long.

The scene that followed was like a choppy Keystone Cops episode. I yelled orders while Scott scoured the closet for what would now be our "do-it-yourself birth kit" since the midwife was thirty minutes away in good weather.

Daddy got on the phone to the midwife, relayed messages to Mother, who hollered them to Scott, who attended to me. In the meantime, Rachel took careful notes in the section of her loose-

leaf organizer entitled "Things I Must Never Do." Then she dived in like a trouper, ready to boil rags or tear up sheets.

When our daughter arrived, we named her Rachel, after one of my favorite people in the whole world: my sister.

On the first day of February 1992, my sister gave birth to her first child—her way. She went into labor after a full night's rest, at about seven in the morning, on her day off. Seven and a half hours later, she called me from the exquisitely beautiful and homelike birthing room at the hospital to tell me in graphic detail about the two painful contractions she had endured before calling for the epidural.

I draw some comfort in wondering if the modern way of giving birth in those beautiful birthing rooms would ever have happened if a generation of Mother Earth devotees had not put their collective Birkenstocks down.

"After that," she reported enthusiastically, "it was great. We all sat around and laughed and played gin rummy." That evening, when I called to check on her and her new son, she could hardly talk because she was chewing steak from the candlelight dinner the hospital had served her and Gilley. She apologized for cutting me short, but she had to call the gym and make her next racquetball appointment before it closed.

Good grief! I mentally ground my teeth. *She has managed yuppie childbirth!*

As memories of my totally natural Lamaze, Laboyer, LaLudicrous births swept over me, all I could think was, *What was I thinking?*

In retrospect, I draw some comfort in wondering if the modern way of giving birth in those beautiful birthing rooms with loved ones about would ever have happened if a generation of Mother Earth devotees had not put their collective Birkenstocks down. Maybe I had a tiny part in helping my sister's childbirth experience be one she will always cherish. I hope so. But I'll tell you one thing for *sure*. If I ever have another baby (heaven forbid, since I'm nearing the big 5-0!), I will be the woman shouting, "Give me all the drugs you've got!"

Then I'm going to sit back, relax, and watch the painless proceedings as I phone my sister and ask her to bring me the juiciest steak dinner she can find.

Chapter 7

Sisters Were Created to Teach Us Patience

Your Best Sweater

If your sister is in a tearing hurry to go
out and cannot catch your eye, she's
wearing your best sweater.

—PAM BROWN

One of a Kind
Martha Bolton

To say my sister, Melva, is one of a kind would be putting it mildly. First and foremost, she has a heart of gold. She has volunteered at homeless shelters and the Red Cross, taken people into her home, and if you're moving, she'll actually get offended if you don't ask her to help you pack.

Melva, though not a licensed counselor, loves to hear people's stories. She used to drive an airport shuttle and would turn the travel time into therapy sessions. She would have total strangers in tears by the time they got to their destination. (I'm not sure if it increased or decreased the size of her tips.) Once she accidentally walked into a fiftieth wedding anniversary party at a hotel, then, realizing what the party was about, walked over and tearfully made the family promise to appreciate their parents while they were still here on earth. Then she left. I guess it was sort of like the Lone Ranger, only without the horse or Tonto. She even attended a funeral once because she was waiting on a bus and had an hour to kill. She walked in and took a seat in one of the pews, heard all about this total stranger's life, and, again, consoled the family afterward.

You'd have to know Melva to understand this behavior. We aren't surprised by it anymore. And anyway, it's not like she had stood in the back of the funeral home passing out her home shopping business catalogs for people to order from on their way out. She only did that at a "viewing" once. And it wasn't in the

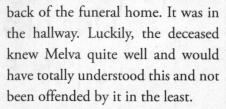

back of the funeral home. It was in the hallway. Luckily, the deceased knew Melva quite well and would have totally understood this and not been offended by it in the least.

Melva didn't think my dad looked "like himself" lying there in the casket.

The funniest funeral story of my sister, though, happened at our father's viewing. Melva didn't think my dad looked "like himself" lying there in the casket. His shoulders were kind of scrunched up, making the position of his head appear unnatural.

She didn't like the way his hands were folded together over his chest either. So she decided to "adjust" him. I tried to tell her to wait and speak to the funeral director about it, but Melva has always been an "I can handle it" kind of person. So she handled it. She "adjusted" my father, pushing his shoulders up, down, this way, and that way, until finally he was in what appeared to be a far more comfortable position. Now it was time to work on his hands. But just as she started to move the hand that was on top, the body had some sort of postmortem muscle reflex, and his hand shot up toward her!

Needless to say, she screamed and went running down the hallway of the funeral home. Having just seen what I saw, I wasn't very far behind!

I believe Melva learned her lesson on that one. Now when she goes to funerals, she leaves the "adjusting" to the professionals.

I'd say that's probably a good idea.

Even when I called her this morning, she made me laugh. She sounded tired, so I asked if I had awakened her. She told me that she was in the middle of delivering newspapers, a route she'd been helping out with lately. We talked a bit, then hung up. A few minutes later, she called back because she was now awake enough to realize that she wasn't out delivering newspapers. She was still in bed. She had just been dreaming she was delivering newspapers.

One of a kind? You'd better believe it!

Where DNA Meets DMV

Rebekah Montgomery

I know it's asking a lot, but I need all of you who have a sister you love to do me a big favor: be kind to people who drive slowly in the left lane.

I know! I know! It can be really aggravating to get stuck behind one of them, but it's important to be nice, and I'll tell you why.

I am not normally an aggressive driver. Honest. And with a few years' distance on the whole incident, I can't even remember what rendezvous with destiny had me driving like my backseat was in flames. But I was in a hurry that day.

Burning rubber along a four-lane highway leading into Fort Wayne, Indiana, I suddenly found myself trapped behind a big old yellow car neatly hogging the left passing lane. The right, slower lane was jammed with cars placidly tooling along, enjoying the bright spring sunshine at the speed limit—or just below

it—but this yellow car was puttering maddeningly slower than that, completely plugging the left passing lane.

Okay. No problem, I thought, pulling behind the yellow car and moving up close.

The driver paid absolutely no attention.

This calls for a little more firmness, I decided.

I turned on my headlights and flashed the brights off and on.

No response.

I honked.

The driver applied the brakes.

Where do these drivers come from? I fumed. *What kind of person blocks traffic in both lanes?*

My right temple began to throb.

While the dashboard clock ticked away, the driver of the yellow car showed indifference to my growing frustration and time schedule. It seemed deliberate. Speed up. Slow down. Every time I had a chance to pass, I was cut off. I couldn't believe it!

I am normally a patient person. Honest. But now I was totally irate with this driver and imagining all sorts of clever things I would like to say, beginning with "Were you sired by a snail? Or a turtle? Or did you get your road hog genes on your mother's side of the family?"

I was totally irate with this driver and imagining all sorts of clever things I would like to say.

What kind of weird genetic mutation produces people who drive in the left lane? I wondered for the next several miles, as I frothed at the mouth and clawed the steering wheel. I was about to find out.

The yellow car leisurely signaled a left turn and pulled into the turn lane at a red light. My window rolled down, I pulled abreast, locked and loaded to give that driver a piece of my mind.

To my great shock, a familiar face looked back at me. It was my sister Rose.

"Becky!" she cried with joy at the sight of me.

My anger deflated.

Rose. One of the most considerate people I know. Sweet as her name, she's generous almost to a fault, has taught Sunday school and children's church for years, and doesn't have a malicious bone in her body. But she has a mental block: She thinks that by driving in the left lane she is "out of the way" of other drivers. And I can't convince her otherwise. Believe me; I've tried.

So out of this experience, I would like to ask all of you who have a sister you love to do me a big favor: Be as kind to the other driver as you would your sister—even when he or she is hogging the passing lane.

That time it was my sister, but next time it could be yours. Or mine. Honest.

The Wedding Glove

Shanna Gregor

I wish some wise woman had taken a moment to tell me that the perfect wedding doesn't exist. Such vital information certainly would have calmed my nerves as my perfect plans escaped me that day.

Looking back twenty years later, it's a comedy. We were late to the wedding. My mother was forever late to everything, and somehow I had agreed to ride with her and Dad to the church. Arriving half dressed, I rushed to get hot rollers out of my hair as my mom tried to help me with my expensive white panty hose etched with tiny white roses. In the frenzy, Mom snagged her ring on my hose, ruining them. One of my girlfriends ran to Wal-Mart and bought plain white panty hose. I was disappointed, but that was just the beginning.

We were late for pictures. My sister Shanae and my cousin Tracey looked beautiful, adorned in powder blue gunnysack

formal dresses. Of course, no one could really tell how gorgeous everything looked because the photographer, a family friend, never turned up the house lights and took all the pictures by candlelight. They were also very distant. None of my wedding pictures have ever adorned the walls of my home for this very reason.

"Blaine and Shanna's getting married—that's so funny!"

Blaine, now my husband, played baseball in high school and college, and all of his teammates thought it would be hilarious to put condoms on the windshield wipers of our "getaway" car. My youngest sister, Jill, freaked out about the condoms, and in tears finally convinced a family friend to remove them.

The train on my dress was so long that my dad, once he gave me away, was unable to step over my dress and sit down with my mother. All the pictures of us standing at the front of the church facing our minister had my dad standing reverently smack dab in the middle of my dress.

As the music stopped and the minister took a breath to begin the ceremony, a small little voice in the audience said, "Blaine and Shanna's getting married—that's so funny!" Stifled giggles erupted as our six-year-old flower girl walked back to the seat where her two-year-old brother was sitting, put her fingers to her lips, and loudly shhh'd him, but not before he said it again—this time clapping his hands.

Arguably the most memorable moment throughout the entire event, however, was when all that love and nervousness in the sanctuary leaked out, oozing onto everyone as we began to

exchange our vows. My bridesmaids were crying, sniffing, and snorting. At one point the minister stopped the ceremony and gave my sister Shanae a minute to compose herself. At that exact moment, the back of her lace-gloved hand went to her nose and she wiped—hand to elbow, the full length of her gloved arm.

Her eyes were wide and I could tell she was holding her breath, not sure what to do. My groom took the lead as the entire wedding party burst into laughter. The tension was broken, and we all sighed with relief.

Over the years we've watched our wedding video—playing and rewinding this specific section for a good laugh at the expense of my good-hearted middle sister.

Hey, Got Any Hershey Bars?

Cathy Lee Phillips

Speaking recently to a civic group, my program dealt with southern delicacies such as cornbread, turnip greens, and Brunswick stew. We laughed and had a wonderful time together, and I immediately felt as though I'd made 150 or so new friends. Imagine my surprise when, as a gift, the group presented me with an unbelievably generous gift certificate to an exclusive five-diamond restaurant. From corn bread to crème brûlée! Could I make the transition? I was up for the challenge!

Because this gift certificate was certainly extravagant enough for two meals, I asked Jennifer Huycke, my best friend and "sister of choice," to go along. Except for the genetics, Jennifer and I are sisters in every way that really matters. We have seen each other through weddings, funerals, tragedies, and triumphs. We act alike, think alike, and—get this—both married United Methodist ministers. The truth is that we look so much alike,

people think we're biological sisters anyway. And, as only a sister can do, Jennifer has a passion and a talent for embarrassing me whenever and wherever she can.

That last point was reason enough for some serious thought before inviting Jennifer to be my dining companion at such a posh restaurant. What if she decided it would be cute to come out of the rest room with her skirt tucked into her panty hose? What if she started snorting or doing impressions of her favorite Disney characters when the waiter took our orders? Dangerous—she knows she can get me with that routine! Or what if she asked for "lavender trout with feng shui sauce and chitlins." It was risky, but I wondered if we would ever have a chance to enjoy such grand cuisine again—so I made the call. Jennifer accepted without hesitation.

I lectured her before we left for the restaurant.

"Please, Jennifer, try to behave tonight. After all, this gift certificate has *my* name on it, not yours. If you cause a scene, it will be me they'll be disparaging after we leave. So, could you please, please keep things under control?" I pleaded.

Of course she promised. Stupid me. I just had to wave that red flag in front of my favorite raging bull!

After a valet I did not know took my keys and my car, Jennifer and I entered the very elegant restaurant known for its French and Mediterranean cuisine. The decor was exquisite, with antiques, fresh flowers, candles, and overstuffed chairs at each perfectly set table. We had a breathtaking view of the city.

Once seated, the very attentive staff described their vintage wines in great detail. We declined and ordered iced tea instead. Our glasses quickly arrived, accompanied by crystal containers holding a clear liquid that, we were told, was melted sugar for sweetening the tea to our desired taste. Fresh lemon was added to the table, and menus were presented to each of us.

I began to breathe again. So far, so good.

As we looked at the menu, Jennifer and I realized that there was an awful lot of food we didn't recognize. We are, after all, preachers' wives more familiar with fried chicken and green bean casserole. "What do you suppose chilled watercress and potato soup would look like?" I whispered. At least I could read that one.

"Nooooooo clue," Jennifer responded, taking another furtive look around.

"Let's order chicken," I suggested. "Chicken is always safe."

We both ordered a dish that had the word *chicken* in it. How the chicken would be prepared or what would come with it remained a mystery—even after it arrived. We quickly agreed that it was muy delicioso!

Once we were finished, we relaxed at our table—by the fire, no less—and drank more iced tea with liquid sugar. Soon the waiter appeared to describe our dessert choices.

"We have a white chocolate soufflé accompanied by an ever-so-delicate Belgian ice cream," he began. "We also have a cherry soufflé complemented by a vanilla kirsch crème anglaise."

My head was spinning!

But, there was more. "Perhaps you would prefer our double chocolate cake served with brandied raspberry sauce, or the fresh fruit tart with just a dab of sweetened whipped cream and grated chocolate. Many clients simply rave about our almond tart served with blueberries and drizzled with a delightful Grand Marnier sauce. And a particular favorite of mine is the cream cheese torte covered with a rich toffee syrup."

The monologue seemed never-ending. There were so many chocolates and soufflés and glazes and sauces that Jennifer was making fish eyes at me across the table. Perhaps it was the stress of the moment or the sense that somehow she had let me down so far by taking the high road to dining etiquette. Perhaps we'd had too much sweet tea or too much hickory smoke from the friendly fire. Something snapped.

"Hey, you got any of them Her-shāy bars?" she asked. "I heared" (yes, she said heared) "them is reeeeeal good."

A certain look came over Jennifer's face—a look I've seen before, a look that usually means I'm about to be mortified.

Yep, my friend, my cohort, my sister, jumped right into the middle of the waiter's dessert monologue, practically shouting, and said, "Hey, you got any of them Her-shāy bars?" she asked. "I heared" (yes, she said *heared*) "them is reeeeeal good."

At that point, I'm sure I heard the waiter say, "Hurumph!"

"I'm sorry, ma'am," he responded. "I believe we are out of chocolate bars."

I couldn't help myself—I laughed—and spewed half of my tea sweetened with liquid sugar and toasted Jennifer with the rest. I looked at Jen and shook my head. How could I be mad at someone so funny and charming, someone so willing to throw pretension to the wind and just be herself? We had had a wonderful time. I felt a rush of gratitude for the ladies who had treated us to such a magnificent dinner. But I was glad to be reminded that Jen and I know who we are, and we're comfortable with that.

True, I was a bit unnerved when she decided to walk out of

the restaurant wearing one heeled shoe and carrying the other, sputtering about how her feet "was a-killin' her." I knew she was eating up the looks she was getting as she clumpity-clumped amid the posh decor. It was exactly what she was going for.

On the way home, we stopped at an Amoco station, and Jennifer plunked two Hershey bars on the counter. "Chocolate—no sauce," she said, handing me one.

Potato Chips and Sister-Friends

Teresa Roberts Logan

I never had a sister. I never wanted one.

I saw all those movies. The ones where the evil sister or step-sister steals your clothes and your man and burns your favorite treasures. Or, worse, feeds you rats or accuses you of murder.

Yes, I'm talking *What Ever Happened to Baby Jane?* and *Hush, . . . Hush, Sweet Charlotte.* Bette Davis surely did her part in my life to make me glad I got a brother instead of a sis.

My friends who had sisters spent their time screaming at them or getting screamed at by them. Not a pretty picture.

But sometimes they let you play with their toys. My friend Beth's big sister, Debbie, let us play with her exquisite Barbie set. We loved her except when she screamed at us for being so uncool. Who cares? She had the Barbie trifecta—furnishings, Ken, and car. There was a sofa with legs and cushions (!), and Ken was really handsome, even if his hair was hard plastic. There were cups and dishes and A NEW CAR! (Read this last part with game show announcer voice.) Beth's sister told us about the birds and the bees. Well, she told Beth and Beth told me. (I didn't believe it for years!)

My friend Teresa (one of two of my best buds named Teresa— yes, there were *three* of us who hung out sometimes!) was a sister-friend. I'm southern, so you must read this "sistuh-free-ind"—three syllables, no less, no more.

Judy burst into tears, hyperventilating, "My sist-she-gah-mad-and-she-spit-and-I-don't-wan-tell-Ma-and——"

My first Teresa-friend was the one who encouraged me to do standup, the one time I ever thought about it—which was in seventh grade. I was yammering on and on (can you imagine?) about whatever I was thinking about at the time, and she was laughing hysterically (much like you are now) and asked me if I had ever thought of doing standup. I said, "Well, yes, *once*." And left that thought in the dust for the next decade and a half. But whenever people ask me if I always wanted to do standup, I say no. Except for that moment with my sistuh-free-ind Teresa.

I think of my best women buds over the years, childhood and on—Beth, Teresa, Teresa, Jennifer, Tania, Kathy, Lea, Marsha, Lisa, Mindy, Dionne, Donna, Donna, Jean, and Molly . . . and I feel really blessed that I've had (and have) sister-friends.

Just *like* sisters. The *good* kind, not the Bette Davis kind. The kind who bring you chocolates, not rats.

That's the kind of sister I wanted. The Hallmark kind. The kind of sister who paints stuff with you and helps you plan surprises and shows you how to put on makeup and dresses up

puppies and rides bikes with you. The kind they have in those fake pictures of families they put in frames to sell at Wal-Mart. The kind who puts her arms around you in the picture for real, not just to do "devil horns" behind your unsuspecting head.

Of course, even the ideal sisters can become temporarily homicidal. Like the time Judy and Lisa (sister-sisters) had a crush on the neighborhood cute guy. I never understood this, because, unfortunately for us, the neighborhood cute guy was a bully with a vicious dog. Just like in the movies!!! But, hey, I wasn't one to judge. But I do have a weak stomach, which brings me back to the sister story.

I'm sitting out front playing with my poodle, Angel (I'm not kidding), and Judy came walking over. She wasn't running or agitated. More like downtrodden. We talk a minute while I'm holding Angel and making her paws do patty-cake (dogs *love* that!), and I didn't know anything was up until I looked up at Judy's face.

"Isn't she cute, Judy? The vet did her nails, which is so prissy, but it's really cute, I think, and I like playing with her out here because she barks at me inside the house and I really don't under-stand that, do y—

"Oh my gosh, Judy, what happened to your face?"

Judy burst into tears, hyperventilating. "My sist-she-gah-mad-and-she-spit-and-I-don't-wan-tell-Ma-and—" which I barely registered, fascinated and disgusted by whatever was all over her face.

"Judy, *what* is *that*?!!"

"PO-TA-TO CHIIIIIIPS!!!" she melted into a full-on Lucy cry.

Turns out her sister, mad that Judy liked the same guy, and with the same sensibility it took to like the bully in the first place,

had chewed up potato chips and spit them all over Judy's face. Now, you're probably wondering the same thing I was.

"Well, that *is* gross, Judy, but why is it still on your face?"

"I—*don't*—*know*. BWAAAAAAAHHHH."

"Well, calm down, we'll go inside and I'll—my mom—will wash your face off. Good grief, Judy."

Judy was a sister-friend. Her sister Lisa *wasn't*.

Picture these sisters running through a field together. Uh-oh, there's only one man to meet them. Let the fireworks begin. Back to Bette-Davis-sister. Hide the hatchets. And the potato chips.

I never did understand why Judy walked around half the morning with chewed-up chips on her face. For sympathy?

When you have a brother, you learn early to stay just beyond spitting distance. This knowledge must come later with sisters. My brother would've been wearing those chips this fast if he had tried anything like that on me.

Did I mention my brother? How much I love him? How thankful I am for him?

I will break to apologize at this point to all of you women who have great sisters and healthy relationships with them, who don't remember fighting or getting angry over tattling or clothes-borrowing or man-stealing.

Actually, I won't apologize. You are in La-La Land. Good for you. I want to be in La-La Land, but it is *my job* to point out this stuff, and it is for your own good, and you know it.

Are there *really* sisters who grow up sharing and introducing each other to their friends while they speak *below* ninety decibels and close doors gently and only when necessary?

If I were any kind of detective, I would seek these sisters out. I would start a reality show starring them called *Survivor: Sisters*

Edition or *Sister Hunters* or *Dancing with Sisters*. Forget that last one. It would star Hugh Jackman as the host because—well, do you really have to ask?

Most sisters I know are grown-ups now. They like to reminisce about the great times when they were kids. I (being the optimist, as you might have guessed) point out the heinous screaming times and the times doors were slammed in our faces. Oh yeah, they say. Thing is, time has healed the sisters' relationships.

These are what I call the "evolved sisters." The Hallmark Sisters. I'm glad they count me as one of their own.

Chapter 8

Sisters Reside in a Town Called Disaster

DISASTER
POPULATION
257~~3~~ 2
ENTER AT YOUR OWN
RISK

The Crabgrass of Life

Big sisters are the crabgrass in the lawn of life.

—CHARLES M. SCHULTZ

Decorating Duo Run Amok
Tina Krause

My sister-in-law and I are "sisters" in every sense of the word. We love doing things together and look forward to those times when my brother Marshall—Jackie's husband—and my husband are out of town on business.

Last time that happened, Jackie invited me over to see the guest room she had just redecorated. I fancy myself a bit of a decorator as well, so I was excited to see what she had done. As expected, it was way beyond lovely. The guest room resembled the cover of *Decorating Dreams*—a most amazing mix of comfort and elegance.

As I passed through the hallway back to the living room, however, I glanced into Jackie and Marshall's bedroom and paused.

"Hum," I said with chin in hand, "Your bed is so pretty and I love your wall color, but the bed linens don't do the room justice."

"Really?" she responded with interest.

"Yeah, I'm sure we could find linens that would make the wall color pop while giving the room a richer, more sophisticated look," I said, waving my hands with the flourish of an interior designer.

"You want to go shopping?" she offered.

I arched my eyebrows. "Sure, maybe we can find a comforter on sale."

Big mistake! With the guys gone, the two of us had nothing better to do than allow our "creative" juices to flow—or should I say "over" flow.

Typically, Jackie and I decorate on a budget. But this time was different. Somehow, our shopping excursion quickly escalated into a buying frenzy, one selection leading to another and another and yet another! We were soon completely out of control.

We found the rich-colored bedding we were originally seeking—the rightness of it bringing a flush of excitement to our faces. We placed it in the cart, and then—

"Look," Jackie said, "these rattan nightstands would go great with the bedding."

"Let's check out the lamps," I said, darting for the lighting department. I could already feel my adrenaline flowing and my blood running hot. "Hey!" I announced, "these lamps are perfect with the rattan, and how about those accessories?" I said, pointing to a nearby shelf. We loaded the shopping cart and raced to the front of the store to get another one.

"Tina?" Jackie clamored at one point, after I scurried in another direction. "Where are you?"

I peeked around the corner of the bathroom aisle. "You won't believe what I found!" I said, waving a shower curtain that

matched the comforter. "It's perfect for your master bathroom! Am I right?" Next, I grabbed the coordinating soap dispenser, shower rings, and tissue holder as Jackie giggled in reckless abandon.

"We'll be needing bath towels, at least four hand towels, and maybe a half dozen washcloths and a bath mat," she exclaimed, pointing like a crazy woman at some nearby displays.

Somehow, our shopping excursion escalated into a buying frenzy. We were soon completely out of control.

Two overflowing shopping carts later, we found ourselves at the checkout.

Cha-ching! Dramatic pause and "That will be five hundred seventy dollars, please."

We stared at each other in shock and awe, and Jackie began to bite her fingernail.

Shaking off impending guilt, we attempted to squeeze our finds into Jackie's Volkswagen Beetle.

"Forget it—all this stuff isn't going to fit," Jackie said, frustrated.

"Sure it will," I assured her as we tipped, rearranged, and shoved in the items tighter than garbage in a trash compacter. We drove away with me perched on the passenger seat, my face kissing the windshield.

Almost exactly one hour after Jackie dropped me off at my house, she called.

"What in the name of heaven were we thinking?" she said flatly. "It's got to go back—*all of it*—and before Marshall gets home!" she bawled. "You're going to have to help me!"

For the second time, we loaded all the bed and bath frills and thrills into the tiny Volkswagen—which I must say holds considerably more than one would imagine—and headed for the store.

The checker stared at us in disbelief as we carted our returns inside. Perhaps it was her glassy stare or the hard set of her chin, but something suddenly seemed *very* funny. Our shoulders shook and our eyes danced as we stifled our snickers and shot each other amused glances. Our patient clerk never seemed to notice as she stoically reversed the sale on each item. On the way home, we laughed so hard our sides ached, brainstorming ideas about what we should say when our husbands asked what we had been doing while they were away. Joyriding?

Jackie and I still love to do things together, but we are "owning" our unfitness as "shopping buddies." In the future, we plan to pursue other common interests—ah, like dieting perhaps?

Exploding Bakery

Shanna Gregor

My sisters and I love bread. As children we were thrilled when Mom went to the Wonder Bread store and bought fresh loaves. We ate it right out of the bag, carefully pulling away the crust and rolling it up in a ball so that it looked like a mini cinnamon roll. Then we would flatten the roll, pull off strips, and pretend we were eating pizza dough.

I have grown up to be an absolutely terrible cook, so I was thrilled to discover how easy it is to make fresh-baked bread from frozen dough available in the freezer section of my grocery store. My husband and I had just purchased our first home, and I was so excited to impress my sisters with my ability to bake "homemade" bread. My younger sister, Jill, and her husband; and my middle sister, Shanae, and her boyfriend were driving from Tulsa to our home in Fort Worth to spend Easter weekend with us. They were scheduled to arrive about 6 p.m.

The bread required six hours to thaw, so I took it out of the freezer that morning and placed each roll of dough into a baking pan and set them on top of the refrigerator. I planned to slip them into the oven after I picked my boys up from school so the house would smell like a bakery when my sisters arrived.

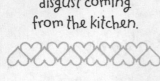

I was awakened by screams of disgust coming from the kitchen.

I'm a shameless pretender, I thought to myself with a smile!

I spent the rest of the afternoon cleaning house and preparing for the family get together. (My parents were already there.) My sisters arrived, and we got down to the serious business of catching up, conducting a tour of the house, pointing out the virtues of our spacious yard, and even taking a stroll through the park across the street.

"Location, location, location," I glammed, doing nothing at all to stifle the growing sense of pride I was feeling.

A few hours later, we all sat down to a wonderful meal prepared by my husband. As always, it was amazing. Not once did I remember the bread rising on top of the refrigerator.

The next morning, I was awakened by screams of disgust coming from the kitchen. Jill had gotten up and opened the refrigerator to get the creamer out for her coffee. By the time I got to the kitchen, the whole family was there. Jill was holding her hand up in the air, covered in goo.

"What *is* this?" she kept saying.

"Oops," I said sheepishly. "It's my 'homemade' bread!"

"More like the blob that ate the refrigerator," my dad was quick to add as we all stared at the disgusting remnants hurled up,

down, over, and around by a doughy explosion. It was a world-class mess—the refrigerator front, sides, and top, and the upper cabinet were seriously encrusted.

They say it's not what goes right that people remember but what goes terribly wrong. Ask any of my sisters about that beautiful Easter and it won't be the perfectly baked ham, the lovely green bean casserole, or the scrumptious apple pie they'll remember. It won't be the crocheted tablecloth or the matching candlesticks. Oh no! Either Jill or Shanae will suddenly jump up, point her finger at me, and begin to chortle. "Oh my goodness, I remember that Easter. Shanna's bread blew up!" Then they'll start laughing those loudmouthed, full-faced guffaws that only sisters can appreciate. And me? I'll just have to join them . . . and wait. Eventually, one of them is going to make a mistake—and, trust me, I'll be all over it!

Going, Going, Gone
Martha Bolton

"They're going to give us twenty bucks for it?" I asked my sister, Melva, in disbelief. "Are you sure?"

"They said twenty," my sister repeated. "Thirty if we throw in the old cabinet radio."

"Sold!" we exclaimed in unison, giving each other a high five. We couldn't believe what was happening. All we did was post a sign that said Garage Sale, and our yard was swarming with shoppers. We sold the baby crib I'd long since outgrown, clothes, jewelry, dishes, antique records—whatever we could find around the house that was old and seemingly useless.

Mom and Dad were away on vacation, and we were determined to surprise them with more money than they could ever make in one weekend. Each time the stock on the front lawn ran low, one of us would excitedly return to the house to find more

items to sell. On one trip, we weren't quick enough, and a few of the customers came in after us.

"How much would you take for that two-piece sofa set?" one woman asked.

My sister and I looked at each other. It certainly wasn't new, and Mom had been talking about replacing it. Still, it was our living room furniture. If we sold it, what would the family have to sit on?

"We don't really know if we can sell that," we hedged.

"I'll give you ten bucks for each piece," she coaxed.

"Ten dollars? That would be twenty bucks for the whole set!" We had no idea how much it would cost to replace, but we did know

We were determined to surprise them with more money than they could ever make in one weekend.

another twenty bucks would bring our day's total to over three hundred dollars! Mom and Dad were going to be so proud of us! They were going to be thrilled! They were going to be—

"You did *what*?!" Mom said as walked into the house and saw the empty spaces where the furniture used to be.

"But we made over three hundred dollars," we said as we handed her the wad of bills.

"Do you have any idea what the things you sold were worth?"

Her tone of voice made it hard to tell whether she was laughing or crying. I think a little of both.

"More than three hundred dollars?" we asked meekly.

By our calculations, we'll be allowed to come out of our rooms in just three more years.

River Scarf

Teresa Roberts Logan

I grew up in Memphis, Tennessee, on the Mississippi River, smelling the barbecue and watching the cotton bales get piled up on the downtown sidewalks ready to be loaded and sent downriver. My Southern Baptist church would always do these riverboat dinners. And my sisters in Christ (and potlucks) and I were always there.

It sounds much more romantic than it is. I pictured Mark Twain lookalikes and handsome gambler types and red velvet Victorian settees. Something like the Cunard Line would've provided, circa 1912, with a grand staircase where I could enter to impress the crowd.

The sistren and I dressed up—we actually thought up what outfits we were going to wear and excitedly discussed them at Youth Group on Wednesday night.

The sistren were very free with their advice: "Teresa, you cannot

wear that purple dress. You wore that to the Donny Osmond concert and everyone remembers it."

"Well, I can't wear the thing I wore to choir or the what-chamacallit I wore to the banquet!" (Do Baptists ever tire of our food gatherings? I say *no*.)

"If you wear that purple thing with that red sweater, that would change it."

"Purple and red clash, and you know it. I am *not* wearing that."

Truth was, I really didn't care that much—I just liked talking about it.

Truth was, we needn't have concerned ourselves in dressing up for *this* riverboat.

This was more like a floating Baptist Fellowship Hall/red metal parade float. There were weathered benches, exposed rusty pipes, and red linoleum to complete the picture.

The sisters and I were a bit disappointed in the digs, but glad as usual to be hanging out with each other.

We had pictured a seafood buffet brought up from N'awlins, where we could dine on crab legs, shrimp cocktail, and hush puppies to our hearts' delight, after which would follow a sumptuous presentation of bananas Foster. What we received was watery spaghetti, a Baptist potluck staple,* and brownies for dessert, while a bossy "captain" yelled at us to not be "lollygaggin' 'round the rails, 'cause if you fall over the side and drown, we are not stoppin'!"

There was no Department of Homeland Security in *those* days. Nope, you were on your own.

*No resemblance or disrespect to Baptist meals, living or dead, is implied or should be inferred.

I had dressed nicely, in the purple dress, and carried a nice little handbag. I am an accessories-aholic, after all. (I just bought a little scarf from a friend who imports things from China. It's lime green, and although the word *mink* was mentioned when the transaction was made, my husband swears it's rat.)

I salivated on the shore in the darkness, waiting for the glorious evening on the river. I tired of watching for the boat to pick us up on shore, and wandered away from the group. (The particular phrase "wandered away from the group" usually is a precursor to graphic scenes in horror movies, but calm down, there is no maniac in this story.)

These river squirrels were not skittish like the ones I encountered on campus; they were downright confident!

I stood on the sloping cobblestones, looking at the huge chains anchored into them for mooring all sorts of river vehicles, and pictured in my head (as opposed to, say, in my elbow) how I would draw them. I observed how the river mud and water covered and shined the cobblestones so there were interesting patterns all over the ground. I went along, looking at the various shapes and thinking of the erasers, pencils, and paper I would bring in daylight to execute a proper drawing, when I saw one of the cutest sights ever—several little squirrels, at night of all things, standing near the edge of the water!

I wonder if squirrels ever swim, I thought, and I was excited to witness something that heretofore modern science may have completely overlooked! I got as close as I could. These river squirrels were not skittish like the ones I encountered on campus; they were downright confident!

Then they turned to look at me with their beady, cute little eyes. Only they weren't squirrels. I was standing, way too close, to big beady-eyed river rats. And they were looking at me. And there weren't three of them, there were hundreds, standing on their haunches in deceptive squirrel-like fashion, and when the light from the approaching riverboat became brighter behind me, I stood staring as thousands of little rat eyes turned toward me in the light. Thousands of little vermin eyes shining towards me in some sort of Spielberg scene, only I didn't have a spaceship, I had a little handbag and Donny Osmond's favorite dress.

All I could think was I must look like Frankenstein's monster to them. Or Gulliver. And I wasn't going to wait around for them to figure out they waaaaay outnumbered me or how creative they could be with rope, rocks, and teeth.

Yep, come to think of it, I've never ever seen squirrels at *night*.

I turned heel and ran as fast as I could to the waiting riverboat and my fellow less adventurous hungry teenagers. "I wandered away from the group, I wandered away from the group!" I was picturing them on my heels, thousands of them, and rats did chase me for a bit, but by the time I got to the group, heaving, "RATS! RATS! RUUUUUN!" and ready to tell my tale of horror, woe, and impending doom (not to mention a movie deal or two if we weren't *completely* devoured), there was nary a rat in sight. No one moved, except slowly toward the watery spaghetti meal. My friends shrugged at me, looking at the empty cobblestones behind me. My nonfriends smirked and proceeded to ignore me. I think I heard one say with disdain, "She's a writer. And didn't she wear that dress to the Donny Osmond concert?"

I had just had a major brush with death! With being eaten

alive! Hadn't they seen *Willard*?! Looking back toward the anchor chains and shuddering, I pictured the hungry river rats (Olympic swimmers, no doubt) following the riverboat cruises every Friday. I saw them waiting for that lone clumsy hapless teenager, full of ennui, who went to the rail to ponder his lonely existence, or just his math homework, and stare at the outline of the Mississippi River Bridge in the darkness.

Slip, splash, dinner is served, and that Bubba guy "ain't stoppin', no way, no how!" I guess I'm glad to have a rat scarf.

It's payback time.

Creepy Crawlers

Karen Scalf Linamen

Harald called me yesterday with a story that will send any arach-niphobics reading this story into therapy.

Harald is my brother-in-law. He and my sister Renee live in Oak Harbor, Washington, with their three boys, six goldfish, and a tarantula.

The tarantula is a new addition. One week ago, their family roster did not include a spider the size of carry-on luggage.

It all started when Renee decided to go away for the weekend. She was going to a women's retreat. As she was heading out the door, her husband announced that he would be taking the boys to the pet store because seven-year-old Hunter wanted to buy a pet. Harald added, "He wants a tarantula."

Absolutely no tarantulas," Renee said. "If a spider like that ever got loose in the house, I'd have to move into a hotel. And I'm not talking Best Western, either. I'm talking Hilton."

The next day Harald and the boys were driving in the van, Hunter cradling a glass terrarium on his lap, when Harald said, "Oh, yeah. Don't let it get loose in the house or Mom'll have to move to a motel or something."

They arrived home and carried their furry friend into the house. Less than an hour later, one of the boys was holding the terrarium when it fell to the floor and broke into tiny pieces. Harald spied the eight-legged wonder sitting dazed among the glass. He rushed to pick it up. The spider promptly bit Harald's finger. Harald flung the spider to the ground, and it scurried under a kitchen cabinet.

Harald looked at the clock.

Renee was due home in two hours.

Armed with a flashlight and broomstick, Harald probed the small hole into which the black spider had fled. No luck.

Returning from the garage, Harald plugged in a 6.5 horsepower Shop-Vac capable of suctioning the dimples off Joe Namath. But it couldn't dislodge an arachnid from under a cabinet.

Undaunted, Harald headed back to the garage. When he returned a few minutes later, he was brandishing an electric saw.

By now several neighborhood husbands had learned of the crisis and gathered 'round to offer hearty masculine support as, piece by piece, Harald began sawing apart his cabinets. The cabinet floor beneath the sink went first. Then various toe plates. Then bottoms of drawers.

They finally found the tarantula in the last possible section of cabinet.

The furry interloper was safely imprisoned in a borrowed terrarium when Renee walked in the front door.

She immediately asked, "What happened here?"

Harald said, "Why do you ask?"

"There's a seventy-five-pound Shop-Vac sitting in the middle of the living room, that's why. What's going on?"

The men in my sister's life—all four of them, from the mid-lifer down to the preschooler—looked her in the eye and said, "Nothing. Nothing happened. Everything's fine."

Around the corner in the kitchen, the cabinets lay in pieces and sawdust was still settling around the flashlights, saws, and Shop-Vac attachments.

I imagine Renee was about to figure it out on her own.

She didn't have to. Hunter confessed. Then, to make up for all the commotion his pet had caused, he decided to do something extra special for his mom.

He named the spider in her honor: "Mama."

We can learn a lot from this story. We can learn to avoid women's retreats, staying home instead to protect our homestead from well-meaning husbands and venomous spiders larger than most of our body parts.

Renee says that the experience is also teaching her to face her fears. She says, "I don't want to steal Hunter's joy over this pet. So I'm working on putting aside my fears. I make a conscious effort to go look at the tarantula at least once an hour, sometimes twice, just to desensitize myself. Not to mention to make sure he's still in his cage."

He named the spider in her honor: "Mama."

Sort of like living with Hannibal Lecter.

Life's like that, isn't it? Sometimes our worst fears come home to roost. Sometimes someone leaves, or someone dies, or the

stock market crashes, or the doctor clears his throat ominously before delivering the news, and like Job in the Old Testament we think, "Here it is. This is it. The thing I have feared has come upon me."

And then we get on with the business of coping, which includes—but isn't limited to—activities like crying and whining, which eventually, if we're lucky, begin to morph into other things like accepting and trusting and growing.

My sister and I wish we could protect ourselves and those we love from everything scary. Instead, we have a God who says, "Yes, sometimes life is scary, but hold my hand and we'll face it together."

And who knows? When it's all said and done, maybe we'll come out ahead, in possession of things we couldn't have gotten any other way, things like mettle and strength and spirit. Not to mention an eight-inch-long spider named Mama.

Snickerdoodles

Shanna Gregor

My mother-in-law is a fabulous baker, but, sadly, both her boys married women who are prone to creating huge disasters in the kitchen. My sister-in-law, Debbie, decided no matter what the cost, she would learn how to make her husband, Dale's, favorite cookies—snickerdoodles.

She found the recipe book our mother-in-law had given her, shopped for the ingredients, and carefully and precisely followed all the instructions.

She tasted the dough, and later tasted the cookies. She couldn't quite figure out why her husband loved these particular cookies so much. She thought they were awful. When Dale came home from work Debbie proudly presented her masterpieces. Dale wolfed them down, pretending to enjoy every last bite, even though they didn't taste at all like his mother's version of his favorite cookie. Encouraged by her husband's enthusiasm, she made Snickerdoodles a regular treat.

After a while, Debbie felt she had this recipe mastered. She was brave enough to bring them to a family gathering. Her husband's secret was out when his mother, Carolyn, picked one up and took a big bite.

> Her husband's secret was out when his mother, Carolyn, picked one up and took a big bite.

"Okay, Debbie, I give up," she said. "What on earth did you put in these cookies?"

"I always follow your recipe," Debbie answered with a smile. "Dale just loves them."

Carolyn wasn't buying it, though.

"Hum . . . show me the recipe, Deb. I'm intrigued by the interesting flavor I'm tasting."

Together they went over the ingredients one by one—and yes, it was her mother-in-law's prized recipe.

Still Carolyn was dubious.

"Can you show me your ingredients?" she asked.

The mystery was solved and the room exploded when they got to "cream of tartar." Deb proudly reached into the fridge and pulled out tartar sauce!

We both learned something that day. You see, like Deb, I didn't know the difference between tartar sauce and cream of tartar.

Once Carolyn filled us in, Debbie looked up at her husband sheepishly and then threw her arms around him. "What a man!" she said. "Eating all those cookies and pretending they were good just to protect my feelings."

Ruth and the Duck

Rebekah Montgomery

"You can't tell," my sister Ruth whispered in the phone.

Since we were little girls, we had kept each other's secrets, but this one was a whopper.

"How am I going to explain this," she wailed. "What am I going to do?"

"Let me think for a minute," I told her. "We'll figure a way out of this."

This one was going to require a lot of thinking. How was she going to explain to her husband why his spanking new Mercedes had a broken grille and the interior was festooned with blood, feathers, and duck doo-doo?

It all started with Ruth's tender heart. Her neighborhood in southern Florida was duck-infested and they freely swam in the canals crisscrossing her neighborhood. Ruth regularly fed them and tried to protect them during hurricanes.

Earlier that afternoon, her husband reluctantly let her use his four-wheeled pride and joy to run errands. She hadn't gone more than a few blocks when an airborne duck flew straight into the grille of the car. (What are the odds!) She ground to a halt and leaped out. The grille lay shattered on the ground. Entangled in it was a bleeding, unconscious duck—the only movement being a pulse pounding in its neck.

Perhaps, she thought, if she could get it to the veterinarian, it might be possible to save its life.

Tenderly, she laid the injured and traumatized duck on the floor mat of the front passenger side of the Mercedes and began to make her way to the "duck"—er—"animal" hospital. As she pulled onto a highway clogged with bumper-to-bumper traffic, an afternoon thunderstorm raged overhead—typical for Florida. Temporarily distracted by the weather and kamikaze drivers, Ruth took her focus off the duck for a few moments.

Increasingly agitated, shedding feathers, and lacking proper toilet comportment, the duck circled the interior of the car.

In a blinding downpour with drivers around her tempting eternity, the duck chose that moment to open its eyes. It shook its head and blinked several times as if awakening from a bad dream. Then, finding itself in a strange place with its wings still functional, it decided to resume its interrupted flight. Quacking indignantly, it flew to the back window and hit it with a crack. Dazed but still on the wing, it made a 180-degree turn and headed for the windshield. This, too, proved to be futile.

Increasingly agitated, shedding feathers, bleeding, and lacking

proper toilet comportment, the duck circled the interior of the car, occasionally chastising Ruth with beak and wing for putting it in an undignified circumstance.

Ruth was frantic too. Not only was she simultaneously being flogged by a duck and narrowly avoiding other drivers, she was going to have to explain all of this to her husband, who did not share her love of all things living.

The next highway exit provided escape. She pulled over and opened the door. The indignant duck flounced forth without a backward glance at his would-be rescuer, leaving Ruth to contemplate the comparative merits of a hard heart.

Well . . . you can see that this was some kind of a devilish duck dilemma my sweet sister was in.

After discussing her options, Ruth put the broken grille in the trunk and took the Mercedes to the car wash to have the interior cleaned and detailed. When they were finished, it looked fine, but the new-car smell was replaced by a strange, rather duckish odor.

Her husband was distressed about the grille. But hey, what's a person to do if a duck flies in front of your car? The rest would be our little secret.

Sometimes when they're out for a ride, though, Ruth's husband will sniff the air with a baffled look on his face. "Does the car smell funny to you?" he asks.

"Yes," she replies each time. "It does smell funny."

Chapter 9

Sisters Are Always in Your Hair

That's My Sister

"Hey! What do ya think you're doin'?
That's my sister.
   "No one's allowed to twist her arm,
push her around, scare the pants off her,
or cut her hair but me!"

—TRUDY TRUMAN

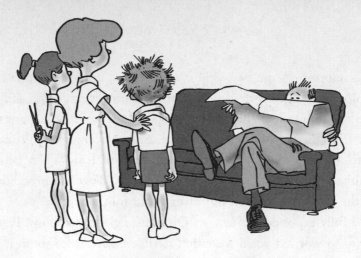

Facts of Life

Patricia Mitchell

You can depend on your big sister to tell you the facts of life. Well, those facts too, but I'm talking about other, more important, facts. I could rely on my big sister, Janice, to let me in on everything I needed to know.

"The fact is," she announced way back when I was an artless twelve and she a cool nineteen, "you need to get your hair cut." With her thumb and index finger extended—the way you approach something that has cooties—she lifted my ponytail and pulled the tip of it around so I could see. "Do you want to wear a ponytail for the rest of your life?" In her other hand, she held a pair of utility shears.

My future flashed in front of my eyes. Eighth grade . . . high school . . . college . . . *my wedding day* . . . with a ponytail hanging down my back! Into the wastebasket landed that suddenly horrific rubber band. I marched into the hair salon (the bathroom)

and hopped on the beautician's chair (the commode), eager for Janice to change my destiny forever. Chunks of brown hair slid to the bathroom tile. While Janice snipped, I pictured myself emerging from the bathroom transformed into a blooming sophisticate with a layered, lacquered, and stylish head of hair. When Janice finished, she held up a mirror so I could see. Wow! We proceeded to the kitchen to present ourselves to our mother.

I fully expected her to say, "Oh, I'm so glad! You know, Patty, I was so worried you'd wear that terrible ponytail for the rest of your life. Why, Janice, you're so thoughtful!" But no—

"What did you do?" she screamed.

"I cut her hair," Janice replied with a measure of pride in her voice. "She's not a little girl anymore." My sister's ability to stand up for herself in the face of our mother's mounting ire impressed me. I, on the other hand, cringed. Mommy marched us both in front of our father, who until that moment was sitting on the sofa and reading his newspaper in peace.

"Look!" our mother hollered. "Just look!" There we stood. I don't know if Janice wavered any, but I was beginning to doubt the wisdom of our project. Papa looked, muttered something unintelligible, and hoisted the paper between his line of vision and the sight of my denuded head.

That night I lay in the dark and hoped everything had been a bad dream. I'd wake in the morning with all my hair right back where it used to be. I'd brush it out, gather it up in one hand, and reach in my dresser drawer for a rubber band with the other—a ritual I expected to carry out for the rest of my days. But the morning enlightened me on another fact of life: some decisions aren't immediately reversible.

Did Janice hone her hair-cutting skills and become a beauti-

cian? No. She became a school teacher and, from everything I hear, an excellent one. Stands to reason: She knows her facts. She dispenses them with the voice of authority, probably because of all the early practice she had with me. I, on the other hand, became a greeting card editor. I specialize in hiding, disguising, and glossing over facts no one really wants to hear.

It's really too bad Janice swerved away from the business of hairstyling. I wore my hair short for the next twenty-five years, and I could have saved a great deal of money if she had offered me free haircuts in some upscale salon. But then in my late thirties, I let my hair grow

My sister's ability to stand up for herself in the face of our mother's mounting ire impressed me. I, on the other hand, cringed.

out. I wanted my ponytail back at the time the women in my age group started lopping off their tresses, deciding, perhaps, that they wanted to look like adults after all. I just smiled at such foolishness and acquired an impressive collection of ribbons, bows, barrettes, scarves, and, yes, rubber bands.

"You look like an aging ballerina," Janice announced, letting me in on a fact I already suspected. A big gap yawned between the elegant coif of my imagination and the testimony of my mirror—and now my sister. Eventually, I reverted to short hair. Janice didn't cut it, though. I made an appointment at an upscale salon.

Lest you think I simply go along with whatever Janice states as fact, let me say, "No way." See, after both of us grew up in California and she married and moved to Texas, we ended up living on two adjacent lots in Missouri. (Go figure.) Proximity,

while a happy thing for the family, gives her day-to-day opportunity to keep me up-to-date on the facts of my life. There's the business of the stray cat, for example.

Early this summer, a beautiful white, silver-tipped, neutered male selected our yards to call home. We asked around the neighborhood, but no one claimed the cat and no one came forward to adopt him. Since four cats already lived with me and two with Janice—and with one longtime stray between us—we agreed the white cat should go to the shelter. She called for a drop-off appointment, and I agreed to take him there. On the drop-off day, I named him Snowy and took him to the vet for shots.

"It's simply ridiculous to have five cats," Janice said as she slipped me a check for half of the vet bill.

Yes. My sister knows the facts of life.

My "Hair-Brained" Extreme Makeover

Brenda Fassett

The summer I turned eight started out normal enough. My sister, Sheila, seven, and I had finished our school year at the end of May. We were giddy with the prospect of long days of play and high adventure. The fact that I had an early June birthday was the icing on the cake. Cake indeed! And ice cream! And presents! Within days, my aunt Charlotte arrived with a small swimming pool in tow. We knew life didn't get any better than this. But after a few days of swimming and splashing, we began to get an itch to do other things—like playing with our "old faithful" toys.

Sheila and I pulled out our tried-and-true Barbie and Midge dolls. We each had one doll. Midge was my favorite. She had beautiful long auburn hair styled in a permanent pageboy. Sheila had a classic blonde ponytailed Barbie.

Then I came up with a brilliant idea, sort of an extreme make-over! I was so excited I could barely speak.

"Sheil," I squealed, "let's make Barbie wigs!"

"Barbie wigs? What do you mean?" she asked.

"Let's make wigs for our Barbies so they can have new hairdos. It'll be great!"

"How do you make Barbie wigs, Brenny?"

"It's easy. You take some hair and put it on the doll's head, okay?" I was about to burst with excitement!

"Where do we get the hair from, Bren?" my little sister asked innocently.

"Well, I guess we'll have to use yours," I answered.

Sheila's eyes flew open, and her face turned white. "My hair? Why my hair? Why not your hair?" she demanded.

"Well, we can use my hair, but do you know how to cut hair for wigs? I've got a pretty good idea how to do it. Do you?"

Her shoulders slumped. She knew my advanced age and superior skills had her beat.

"How much hair?" she asked as she stroked her shoulder-length hair.

"Not much," I replied.

"Mom will know," she said matter-of-factly.

"I'll just take a little from the back. She won't notice."

"You really, really know how to make Barbie wigs, Brenny?"

"Yes," I said, lying unashamedly.

I got the scissors and went to work. I cut, and I cut, and I cut some more.

Before long there was a lot of hair on the floor. It wasn't hanging in nice straight sections like Sheila's haircut anymore. It was just a pile of hair. A big, messy mishmash pile of hair. A no-rhyme-or-reason pile of hair.

Then I looked at Sheila's head. I was aghast. Most of her hair

from the back of her head was gone! How had I cut it so short? How had I cut so much? Suddenly, an overwhelming truth began to surge through my brain—*this is a really, really, really bad idea!*

Sheila turned around and looked down at all her hair on the floor. With the hopeful eyes of a trusting little sister, she held up a fistful of her hair. "So, how do we make it into wigs, Brenny?"

That moment is forever emblazoned in my mind. I had let my sister down before, but this was the first time I had blown it in such a big way. How would I answer her question?

"I don't know," I admitted.

What do you mean you don't know? You said you knew how!" she cried.

"I thought I did."

"You said you did!"

"I thought I did."

Sheila felt the back of her head and started to cry. I didn't have enough sense to cry. But I had a plan. I convinced my sister that if she stayed in the swimming pool all day, Mom wouldn't notice her hair because it would be wet. Sheila ran for the pool, where she submerged her head and stayed wet for the remainder of the afternoon.

"So, how do we make it into wigs, Brenny?"

At suppertime, a waterlogged Sheila was ordered out of the pool. Mom saw her hair. We confessed to the crime and were given our

sentence. Sheila would have to have a very short haircut to "fix" the mess I had made, and I, as the originator of the idea, would

receive the same haircut. And so it was that the two oldest sisters both had fashionable "pixies" for the summer of 1965.

I meekly asked Sheila to forgive me for talking her into such a bad idea. She put her arm around me and said, "It's okay, Brenny. It will be fun to have the same haircut this summer."

That wasn't the last wild idea I dreamed up, but over time, I learned the art of "looking before leaping." I also learned that if you're going to plan a "hair-brained" scheme, there's no better person to bring along for the ride than your sister.

Saved from the Brush

Fran Sandin

"Mom," my daughter had told me, "you might really enjoy using a round brush when you blow-dry your hair. They're great for adding body and bounce." Since my medium-length hair was an odd combination of thick and fine, I was open to suggestions.

The next time I went grocery shopping, guess what? I was thrilled to find a cute, small, round brush for the discounted price of ninety-nine cents. Since I love a good bargain and could envision my hairstyle undergoing a glamorous transformation, I grabbed the beauty tool from the marked-down basket and hurried home to give it a whirl.

As soon as I walked into my kitchen, I plopped down the bag of groceries, turned on the radio, and began humming. While putting cans away in the pantry, I ran across my new purchase and thought, *I wonder how this brush works?* Right where I stood by the kitchen counter, I reached up, grabbed a bunch of hair

from the top of my head, and tucked the strands into the bristles of the tiny brush. Then I began winding. And winding. And winding—while musing, *Hmm, this is just like rolling spaghetti on a fork.* I was amazed at how many turns I could make.

But I was even more surprised when I discovered the brush that had so beautifully wound up my hair now refused to let go. I flew into the bathroom, hoping a mirror would help me see a way to release my locks from the evil contraption. I pulled and tugged in all directions, but my efforts only succeeded in tightening the tangles. My heart skipped a beat as I imagined being stuck with this bonehead attachment forever—like Pebbles from the Flintstones!

Then I remembered Gracie, who lived only a few blocks away. Quickly, I dialed her number. When she answered I stammered, "Gracie, you're my friend, right?—my *really good* friend?"

"Sure," she said reassuringly.

"And as far as you're concerned, we're as close as sisters, right?" I prodded.

"Well . . . yeah," she countered.

"Really, really, really close?" I pushed. "Close enough that you'd be willing to help me out of a jam and keep your mouth shut about it?"

"Come on, Fran. You're starting to scare me. You aren't going to ask me to help you bury a body in your backyard, are you?"

"Of course not, silly! It's a lot worse than that. I'm on my way over. Have the door open so I don't have to knock."

"Yes, but what's the matter?" Gracie persisted at what was now a near shout.

"You'll know when you see me." When I hung up the phone, I felt a combination of urgency and relief. I ran out the door,

jumped into the car, and raced toward Gracie's house like some hair-brained woman.

Considering my delicate condition, I was hoping no one would see me. But while rounding the corner, my hopes were dashed. There stood a rather dignified-looking lady in her designer jogging suit. As I drove by, there was little I could do but smile and wave at her. From my rearview mirror I watched her head slowly swivel in my direction, a curious look on her face. I tried to reassure myself, *Maybe she'll think I'm starting a new trend—"brush-roll-n-go."*

The minute I pulled up to Gracie's sidewalk, she flung open her front door and then burst into laughter as I emerged from the car. "What have you done to yourself?" she asked between loud chortles.

I pulled and tugged in all directions, but my efforts only succeeded in tightening the tangles.

Her response made me want to get back in the car and leave, but I was desperate—so instead I scooted inside, closed the door, and blurted, "Gracie, this is serious! The more I pull, the worse it gets. Can you work on it? Please?"

"Well, let me get the scissors," Gracie quipped with a twinkle in her eye.

"Absolutely not! Are you crazy?"

After a pause of playful hesitation, Gracie said, "You poor baby. Have a seat."

Gratefully, I scooted my chair into place at the kitchen table. For just a moment, I considered insisting we prick our fingers and become blood sisters—at least then she'd be honor-bound to keep my secret. But I quickly realized it was too late for that. I'd

just have to rely on Gracie's natural sense of charity and propriety. The partially stifled chuckles I was hearing behind me did not give me a warm feeling of security.

With tender loving care, Gracie began the arduous task of unwinding the mess of matted hair, strand by strand. Though it sometimes hurt when she pulled, I didn't dare squeal or scream. A little pain was better than the wig I'd have to buy if this operation was unsuccessful. After fifteen or twenty minutes of concentrated effort, punctuated by outbursts of laughter, Gracie triumphantly declared, "Ta-da!"

Then she sang out, "Here's your lovely hairstyling accessory." She gave the brush a dramatic flourish in the air before placing it in my hand. It looked like a hamster that had been caught in a whirlwind.

I immediately put the devilish thing in the trash container under Gracie's sink. Thankfully, only part of my hair was still attached to it. I touched the top of my head and felt the remnants. Breathing a sign of grateful relief, I gave Gracie a big hug and promised I would "be there" if she ever needed me to do anything. Ever. At all.

Later, as I reflected on my emergency, I thought how thankful I was to have Gracie. What would I have done without her? I owe her one—that's for sure! A big one!

Thanks, Sistah Gracie, you saved my day!

Sister Speak
Martha Bolton

There are people in life who don't mince words. My sister, Melva, isn't one of them. Not only does she mince words, she slices, dices, purees, and mixes them. Take for instance the blended word she created today when she was trying to say that something "meant a lot to her daughter" and "it was vintage." The resulting word was "meantage."

She and her children laugh about this quality of their mother's, and one of her sons is even keeping a dictionary of "Melva-speak."

Anyone who knows Melva, though, can usually figure out what she is trying to say. However, there have been a few times in my life when I wished I hadn't been able to follow along. Like the time when she talked me into dressing up like the Easter Bunny and letting her ride me around on the back of her bicycle wishing everyone we passed a happy Easter. Not only was this embarrassing, but it wasn't even Easter.

Another time she talked me into being a mermaid in a school parade. Our dad built the float and had done an excellent job, that is, except for the fact that the wheels didn't turn. That would have been fine had the parade route been like most parade routes and gone in a straight line. But there were several turns along the way that the float was going to have to negotiate. Or not negotiate, as it turned out. The float ended up going off the cement path and into the dirt and getting stuck there. I had no choice but to get off the float and hop in my mermaid tail all the way back to my locker to get my change of clothes. And I wonder why I didn't win a nomination for Most Likely to Succeed come graduation time.

I had no choice but to get off the float and hop in my mermaid tail all the way back to my locker to get my change of clothes.

As embarrassing as both of those situations were, there's one more that has always topped the list for me. Years ago my sister owned a clown business. She would perform as a clown for birthday parties, company picnics, and other such events. One time, however, she couldn't do one of the parties, so she talked me and another friend into filling in for her. The problem was she gave us the wrong address. We drove around for over an hour (that's eternity in clown years) looking for the right house. Finally, she realized the error and called to give us the correct information. But by now we were very, very, very late. The party was almost over when we finally did arrive. Now, it's uncomfortable enough to get the cold shoulder when you walk into a party, but imagine what it would feel like to get it while wearing a clown outfit. A roomful of people mad at a clown

is not a pretty sight. We thought about giving alias clown names and letting Bozo take the wrap, but that wouldn't have been right. So we did the only thing we could do—we apologized and apologized and apologized. In fact, if those people are reading this, I apologize once again.

I love my sister, but now when she tries to talk me into something, I think long and hard about it first. Especially if there's a costume involved. And as for her clown business? She has long since hung up her red nose and oversized shoes. But I'm sure the outfit still holds a lot of good memories for her. I guess you could say it's "meantage."

Contributors

Patti Maguire Armstrong is the mother of ten children ages twenty-five to five, two of whom are brothers who were orphaned in Kenya. She is a speaker and writer who has published around four hundred articles in both secular and religious publications and is the author of five books. Patti is also the managing editor of the *Amazing Grace* book series. Her Web site is www.RaisingCatholicKids.com.

Marti Attoun is a weekly humor columnist for her hometown newspaper, the *Joplin* (Missouri) *Globe*, and has published hundreds of articles in regional and national publications, including *Reader's Digest, Redbook, Christian Science Monitor,* and *Family Circle*. She is also a contributing editor for *American Profile* magazine and writes for *Ladies' Home Journal, Family Circle, Good Housekeeping,* and other national magazines

Martha Bolton is a former staff writer for Bob Hope, two-time

Angel Award recipient, Emmy nominee, and the author of more than thirty books, including *Didn't My Skin Used to Fit?* and the *Official* book series.

Deena C. Bouknight writes for consumer and trade publications in home furnishings, architecture, and decorating, as well as for general interest and regional magazines. She has completed one literary novel, *Broken Shells*, and one children's book, *Our Wintry Day Walk* (Trafford). E-mail Deena at dknight865@aol.com.

Patsy Clairmont is one of the founding speakers of Women of Faith, and author of twenty books. Her latest release is *Dancing Bones . . . Living Lively in the Valley.*

Rebecca Currington is the founder and president of SnapdragonGroup Editorial Services, where she marshals a workforce of 450 freelance writers, editors, compilers, reviewers, and proofreaders. Together they typically produce between fifty and sixty scripts per year for Christian publishers around the country. Read more about it at www.snapdragongroup.com.

Susan Duke is a wife, mother, national speaker, and best-selling author or coauthor of fifteen books, including her most personal and recent release, *Grieving Forward, Embracing Life Beyond Loss.* A gifted communicator, she speaks at Christian conferences and at retreats with her unique blend of humor and heartfelt inspiration. Visit her at suzieduke@juno.com or www.suzieduke.com.

Janice Elsheimer is the author of *The Creative Call,* an award-winning book that invites creatively talented people to view their gifts as an invitation to deeper spiritual growth. Her soon-to-be-released second book, *Grounded in the Garden: The Wisdom of Growing Things,* is a collection of inspirational essays about life, growth, and gardening. Visit Janice at www.jelsheimer.com.

Bonnie Afman Emmorey is a speaker-consultant with Speak Up Speaker Services. She teaches communications skills at Speak Up with Confidence seminars, and is helping to launch Speak Up with Hope. For additional information, go to www.SpeakUpSpeakerService.com and www.SpeakUpForHope.com.

Delia Ephron is the author of many books of fiction and nonfiction for adults and children, including *Hanging Up* and *Big City Eyes*. She is also a screenwriter and producer. Her credits include *Sleepless in Seattle, You've Got Mail,* and *Michael*. Her humor, essays, and commentary have appeared in *The New York Times Book Review, The New York Times, Vogue,* and *Rosie*. She lives in New York City.

Brenda Fassett sees every day as another chance to tell a story and have one more cup of coffee. Brenda's testimony includes her steady husband, Doug, and three highly animated children. She has been a seminar and retreat speaker for twenty years, bringing inspiration and biblical talks to life. Brenda enjoys volunteering at her church and her children's school.

Shanna Gregor has served various ministries and publishers to develop books that express God's voice for today. With a passion to see the Truth touch lives through the written word, she continues to serve through the open doors God sets before her. Shanna and her husband, Blaine, reside in Amarillo, Texas, with their two sons.

Nancy Hoag, who currently lives in Montana, is an award-winning teacher and speaker and the author of more than nine hundred articles, devotions, and columns placed in nearly 160 publications. In addition, she has added four nonfiction books to her credits, including *The Fingerprints of God . . . Seeing His Hand in the Unexpected* (Baker Books/Revell).

Becky Freeman Johnson is ecstatically married to Greg; proud mom and stepmom to a lively clan of young adults; and "Nonnie" to her adorable grandbabies. An award-winning, bestselling author of more than two dozen books of inspirational humor, Becky now lives, loves, works, and smiles a lot under blue Colorado skies. Visit her Web site, www.yellowroseeditorial.com.

Carol Kent is a popular international public speaker, a bestselling author, and a former radio show cohost. A dynamic and humorous speaker, she's been a featured speaker at events for women and families. She is the founder of Speak Up with Confidence seminars and the president of Speak Up Speaker Services.

Karen R. Kilby resides in Kingwood, Texas with her husband, David. Karen is a certified personality trainer with CLASServices, Inc., and a regional speaker trainer and speaker for Stonecroft Ministries and has had several short stories published. Please reach her at krkilby@kingwoodcable.net.

Tina Krause is an award-winning newspaper columnist, speaker, and freelance writer of more than 750 columns and magazine articles. She is author of *Laughter Therapy: A Dose of Humor for the Christian Woman's Heart* (Barbour Publishing, 2002), and has contributed to thirteen devotional books. Tina resides in Valparaiso, Indiana, with her husband, Jim.

Vicki J. Kuyper has been a freelance writer for the last twenty years, writing everything from inspirational books to training videos to sheep pun calendars. Vicki resides in Phoenix, Arizona, while her sister, Cindy, lives in Colorado Springs. Despite the miles and the years, they remain close at heart.

Carmen Leal is the author of nine books including *The Twenty-third Psalm for Caregivers* and *The Twenty-third Psalm for*

Those Who Grieve. She is a popular presenter at women's retreats, church groups, conventions, and conferences. Carmen and her husband live in Kailua, Hawaii. To learn more, visit www.carmenleal.com.

Karen Scalf Linamen is a national speaker and the author of nine humorous self-help books for women, including the CBA best-seller *Just Hand Over the Chocolate and No One Will Get Hurt.* Her newest release is *Chocolatheraphy: Satisfying the Deepest Cravings of Your Inner Chick,* in which she takes a witty look at emotional eating. Visit her at www.karenlinamen.com.

Teresa Roberts Logan is a cartoonist and standup comedian who appears as a featured comic on Warner Bros. groundbreaking Christian comedy DVD, *Thou Shalt Laugh.* She makes her home with her husband, Gary, and her son, Andrew, in Virginia, and believes in living by Proverbs 31:25 (NIV): "She can laugh at the days to come." Her Web site is www.LaughingRedhead.com.

Dandi Daley Mackall is an award-winning author of four hundred books for children and grown-ups. Her publishers include Simon & Schuster, Dutton/Penguin, HarperCollins, Harcourt, Random House, DreamWorks, Tyndale House, Tommy Nelson, Zonderkidz, Shaw, Disney, Warner Bros., and Hanna-Barbera. She's a national keynote speaker and has made dozens of appearances on TV, including ABC, NBC, and CBS. Visit her Web site, www.dandibooks.com.

Patricia Mitchell, former editorial director with Hallmark Cards, is a freelance writer and editor specializing in Bible studies and methodology, inspirational articles, and Christian devotionals. Her book of devotions, *Hear My Voice, O Lord,* is due for release in early summer 2007.

Rebekah Montgomery has more than thirty-five years experi-

ence as a Bible teacher. She is a freelance writer, editor, and speaker. She lives in Illinois with her husband of thirty years. Visit her at www.rebekahmontgomery.com.

Lynn Moore writes inspirational and educational material for children and adults. Her first book for children, *Cave Dave* (innovativeKids, summer 2007), is sure to delight young readers. Moore has written for *Focus on Your Child* newsletter, *ParentLife* magazine, *Hopscotch,* and *Highlights for Children.* Follow her column at http://specialneedsparenting.suite101.com/ .

Brenda Nixon (www.brendanixon.com) uses wit and wisdom to empower millions in their child-rearing skills through her book, *Parenting Power in the Early Years,* media interviews, and published articles. She is a popular speaker at child care/parenting conferences, contributing author to twenty books, and is currently writing a book on child discipline.

Cathy Lee Phillips is an award-winning author and popular speaker who writes books sprinkled with her unique dose of humor with a southern flair. Her articles have appeared in Angels on Earth, Guideposts, and Today's Christian Woman, and in publications by Zondervan, Howard Books, Guidepost Books, and The United Methodist Publishing House. Contact her at www.CathyLeePhillips.com.

Nancy Rue is the author of more than one hundred books for adults, teens, and tweens, and has taught English and drama, directed theater for adults and children, and taught workshops on writing and girls' issues across the country. She lives in middle Tennessee with her husband, Jim, and her dog and cat, Rocky and Benjamin. Her sister, Phyllis, lives in northern Florida, and they try to have "sister dates" as often as possible.

Fran Sandin has authored *Touching the Clouds, Encouraging*

Stories to Make Your Faith Soar, See You Later, and *Jeffrey,* and coauthored the best-seller *Courage for the Chicken-Hearted* and its sequel, *Eggstra Courage for the Chicken-Hearted.* Fran is a registered nurse, organist, speaker, and grandmother and lives in Greenville, Texas. Visit her at www.fransandin.com.

Stacie Ruth Stoelting was only fifteen when she wrote her first Christian book' *Still Holding Hands*, dispensing empowerment and inspiration about Alzheimer's. She has sung for President Bush, and celebrities have endorsed Bright Light Ministry at www.brightlightministry.com. Her ministry beams Jesus' bright light worldwide. Critically acclaimed, her writings and programs effervescently encourage!

Source Notes

Chapter 1: Sisters Are There for You in a Pinch

"Make My Day, Doughboy!" by Karen Scalf Linamen. Used by permission of the author.

"Mad About Mood Rings" by Cathy Lee Phillips. Used by permission of the author.

"Get Back in the Saddle, Missy!" by Dandi Daley Mackall. Used by permission of the author.

"In the Clutches of Summer" by Marti Attoun. Used by permission of the author.

"Any Port in a Storm" by Brenda Nixon. Used by permission of the author.

"'Brief' Shopping Mission" by Marti Attoun. Used by permission of the author.

Chapter 2: Sisters Can Be Hazardous to Your Health

"How to Torture Your Sister" by Delia Ephron. Excerpt taken from *How to Eat Like a Child: And Other Lessons in Not Being a Grown-up.*

Copyright © 1977, 1978 by Delia Ephron. Reprinted by permission of HarperCollins Publishers.

"My Sister's Handiwork" by Bonnie Afman Emmorey. Excerpt taken from *Kisses of Sunshine*. Copyright © 2005 by Speak Up, Inc. Published by Zondervan Publishing, Grand Rapids, Michigan. Used by permission.

"You Go First" by Karen Scalf Linamen. Used by permission of the author.

"Case of the Clandestine Carving" by Patti Maguire Armstrong. Used by permission of the author.

"Inner Sanctum" by Karen R. Kilby. Used by permission of the author.

"I Was Once an Only Child" by Rebecca Currington. Used by permission of the author.

Chapter 3: Sisters Are the Perfect Accessory

"The Benefits of Having Blonde Sisters" by Carol Kent. Excerpt taken from *Kisses of Sunshine*. Copyright © 2005 by Speak Up, Inc. Published by Zondervan Publishing, Grand Rapids, Michigan. Used by permission.

"Note to Self" by Marti Attoun. Used by permission of the author.

"She Had Me and She Knew It!" by Tina Krause. Used by permission of the author.

"The Call of the Wild, Cadillac-Style" by Vicki J. Kuyper. Used by permission of the author.

"The Boy on the Sidewalk" by Lynn Moore. Used by permission of the author.

Chapter 4: Sisters Are Born for Adventure

"To Scheme the Impossible Scheme" by Karen Scalf Linamen. Used by permission of the author.

"The Great Adventures of the Tea Sisters" by Susan Duke. Used by permission of the author.

"No Regrets" by Janice Elsheimer. Used by permission of the author.

"Sloshing Sisters" by Stacie Ruth Stoelting. Used by permission of the author.

"A Sisters' Getaway" by Susan Duke. Used by permission of the author.

"My Sister Made Me Do It!" by Vicki J. Kuyper. Used by permission of the author.

Chapter 5: Sisters Make Good Leaning Posts

"'Shear' Survival" by Carmen Leal. Used by permission of the author.

"One Day Off" by Tina Krause. Used by permission of the author.

"Sistership" by Patsy Clairmont. Excerpt taken from *Best Devotions of Patsy Clairmont.* Copyright © 2001. Published by Zondervan Publishing, Grand Rapids, Michigan. Used by permission.

"Laughter Is the *Best* Medicine" by Deena C. Bouknight. Used by permission of the author.

"The Doctor Is Awake" by Karen Scalf Linamen. Used by permission of the author.

Chapter 6: Sisters Are Familiar Strangers

"Me Too!" by Nancy Hoag. Used by permission of the author.

"The Wonders of Identity Theft" by Marti Attoun. Used by permission of the author.

"It's Your Urn" by Nancy Rue. Used by permission of the author.

"Lizard Boots and Wedding Bells" by Vicki J. Kuyper. Used by permission of the author.

"Not Nice—but Interesting" by Patricia Mitchell. Used by permission of the author.

"Birthin' Babies" by Becky Freeman Johnson. Excerpt taken from *It's Fun to Be Your Sister.* Copyright © 2007 by Becky Freeman Johnson. Published by Harvest House Publishers, Eugene, Oregon. Used by permission. www.harvesthousepublishers.com.

Chapter 7: Sisters Were Created to Teach Us Patience

"One of a Kind" by Martha Bolton. Used by permission of the author.

"Where DNA meets DMV" by Rebekah Montgomery. Used by permission of the author.

"The Wedding Glove" by Shanna Gregor. Used by permission of the author.

"Hey, Got Any Hershey Bars?" by Cathy Lee Phillips. Used by permission of the author.

"Potato Chips and Sister-Friends" by Teresa Roberts Logan. Used by permission of the author.

Chapter 8: Sisters Reside in a Town Called Disaster

"Decorating Duo Run Amok" by Tina Krause. Used by permission of the author.

"Exploding Bakery" by Shanna Gregor. Used by permission of the author.

"Going, Going, Gone" by Martha Bolton. Used by permission of the author.

"River Scarf" by Teresa Roberts Logan. Used by permission of the author.

"Creepy Crawlers" by Karen Scalf Linamen. Excerpt taken from *Welcome to the Funny Farm.* Copyright 2001 by Karen Scalf Linamen. Published by Fleming H. Revell.

"Snickerdoodles" by Shanna Gregor. Used by permission of the author.

"Ruth and the Duck" by Rebekah Montgomery. Used by permission of the author.

Chapter 9: Sisters Are Always in Your Hair

"Facts of Life" by Patricia Mitchell. Used by permission of the author.

"My 'Hair-Brained' Extreme Makeover" by Brenda Fassett. Excerpt taken from *Kisses of Sunshine.* Copyright © 2005 by Speak Up, Inc. Published by Zondervan Publishing, Grand Rapids, Michigan. Used by permission.

"Saved from the Brush" by Fran Sandin. Used by permission of the author.

"Sister Speak" by Martha Bolton. Used by permission of the author.